Praise for *From Desperation to Dedication*

"Troy changed himself. As a result, his story will immediately and effectively change every reader. . . ."

—Mark Victor Hansen

Co-creator, #1 New York Times *bestselling series Chicken Soup for the Soul™*

"What an amazing story. I first corresponded with Troy Evans when he was still in prison. My friend, Robert Henry, chair of the NSA Foundation Scholarship Committee asked me to support Troy in his efforts to get a college education and get out of jail. Since then I've followed Troy's life from prisoner and motivated student, to freed ex-con, to aspiring professional speaker, to the main platform at the National Speakers Association annual convention, to loving husband and father, and now to published author. This is a story you don't want to miss. It will change YOUR life, too!"

—Stephen Tweed, CSP

CEO of Leading Home Care

"If you've ever needed proof that people can make drastic, significant, and powerful changes in their lives . . . if you've ever wondered if you could go from where you are right now, no matter how hopeless your situation may seem, to where you want to be . . . if you want to be inspired, uplifted, and encouraged by someone who has known the depths of despair and then rose to almost unimaginable heights . . . read Troy Evans's story! It could be one of the most important books you'll ever read."

—Al Walker, CSP, CPAE

Motivational humorist and author of Thinking Big & Living Large

"Troy Evans is an inspiration. He put himself in a position where most people would simply give up and then did the honorable—and difficult—thing: He took responsibility for his actions and changed his life. In this powerful book, Evans shows us all how to overcome challenges and embark on a positive journey toward our dreams."

—Randy G. Pennington

Author of Results Rule! Build a Culture That Blows the Competition Away

"If you're looking for a role model, look no further. Evans will help you meet your challenges and embark on a journey to your dreams."

—John Hammonds

President of the American Motivational Association and recipient of the Cavett Award given by the Nation Speakers Association for service to the speaking profession

"Troy Evans has written a moving book. His fascinating story of taking responsibility for the bad decisions that made him a bank robber and landed him in prison is inspiring in its honesty. We can all be better for reading and learning from his experiences and insights."

—Mark Sanborn

Author of The Fred Factor: How Passion in Your Work and Life Can Turn the Ordinary into the Extraordinary

"Troy Evans is simply an inspiration! To overcome the odds he has is extraordinary. His new book helps the rest of us overcome the barriers and stumbling blocks we all face in life."

—Laura Stack

Author of Leave the Office Earlier *and* Find More Time, *as well as the upcoming* Up Your Energy

"Considering his past, Troy's rise in the world of motivational speaking is nothing less than spectacular. He's the right man with the right message at the right time. This book is a 'must read'!"

—Jim Hennig, Ph.D.

Author of Negotiating Your Success

"Troy's message is an inspiration, and he shows us how to live a better life by putting things into the proper perspective. His unique story details the hardships he has overcome in life as he lights the spark of ambition in the eyes and minds of his readers."

—Nido Qubein

President of High Point University, and Chairman of Great Harvest Bread Company

"Trying drugs, getting hooked, selling drugs, stealing to get more drugs—few stories tell the story of a promising athlete and upstanding young man falling farther or faster. Even more remarkable is Troy's transformation in prison from convicted bank robber to honor-roll student, great dad, and upstanding, successful citizen. Best yet, it's all true. If Troy can overcome the challenges he set for himself, so can you."

—Tom Lagana

Professional speaker and co-author of Chicken Soup for the Prisoner's Soul

"Troy Evans is amazing . . . to turn such a negative environment into a positive and successful career as a motivational speaker is simply brilliant. The life-changing principles and inspiring personal stories in Troy's book make for a MUST read!"

—Debbie Allen

Author of Confessions of Shameless Self Promoters *and* Skyrocketing Sales

From Desperation to Dedication

From Desperation

An Ex-Con's Lessons on Turning Failure into Success

to Dedication

Troy D. Evans

WITH CHRIS HOLBERT

BenBella Books, Inc.
Dallas, Texas

BenBella Books, Inc.
6440 N. Central Expressway, Suite 617
Dallas, TX 75206
www.benbellabooks.com
Send feedback to feedback@benbellabooks.com

Printed in the United States of America
10 9 8 7 6 5 4 3 2 1

Library of Congress Cataloging-in-Publication Data

Evans, Troy D.
From desperation to dedication : an ex-con's lessons on turning failure into success / Troy D. Evans with Chris Holbert.
p. cm.
Includes bibliographical references and index.
ISBN 1-933771-09-7 (alk. paper)
1. Evans, Troy D. 2. Ex-convicts—United States—Biography. 3. Motivational speakers—United States—Biography. 4. Motivation (Psychology) I. Holbert, Chris. II. Title.

BF503.E96 2006
158.1—dc22

2006032615

Proofreading by Emily Chauviere & Yara Abuata
Cover design by Laura Watkins
Text design and composition by John Reinhardt Book Design
Printed by Bang Printing

Distributed by Independent Publishers Group
To order call (800) 888-4741
www.ipgbook.com

For special sales contact Yara Abuata at yara@benbellabooks.com

To my beautiful wife, Pam—*my encourager, my believer, my best friend, and my lover—I could not have done this without your support.*

To my son, Eric—*the one who never stopped believing in me—your belief fueled my desire.*

To my parents, Mel and Joyce—*you two set the fine example that I would one day follow, and you never gave up on me. Your love and support made me believe in myself.*

To my brother and sister, Greg and Kim—*you held me closest when I needed you the most. Thank you for the chance to be the big brother I never was.*

To my dog, Archibald D. Evans III (Archie)—*you sit under my desk all day long, listening to my ramblings—may I someday be the man you think I am!*

Acknowledgments

I AM SO VERY GRATEFUL to the numerous people who have accompanied and enabled me on the road to becoming a professional speaker, and now an author. My deepest gratitude goes out to:

The late Robert Henry and his family—Marilyn, Patrick, and Brent. Robert was my first mentor, believer, and door opener in this business. His family welcomed me into their home as if I were one of their own—I will always be grateful to you all. And Robert, I look up at you and smile.

To Bill and Marge Johnson. What rough edges Robert didn't polish, Bill worked into something that was at least presentable. I so very much appreciate his honesty and determination—I also appreciate that Marge was there to keep him in line.

To Wynette Marbut, Robert's secretary and my forever friend. I've felt your support and love for so many years. Thanks for believing.

To Steven Cohen and Aaron Chandler, who through their creative juices and technical support have made me look smarter than I am!

To the National Speakers Association—a group that took a chance on me when all others rejected and discarded my dreams. I would not be where I am today if not for the generosity of its members.

To Chris Holbert, the co-author of this book. Her creative genius is the backbone, heart, and soul of this book. Chris, you took my raw material and turned it into something special. Thank you for all of your hard work and persistence. I am, however, relieved that our sessions of you dragging memories out of me are over with!

To Jeff Olson, my literary agent. Your perseverance and enthusiasm in this project were and continue to be contagious to all involved. Your hard work and professionalism are unrivaled and you have been an absolute pleasure to work with.... Thank you!

To Glenn Yeffeth, Leah Wilson, and all the staff at BenBella Books.

Each of you was an absolute pleasure to work with and only through your vision and belief has this book become a reality. Thank you, and I must add that, as a publisher, you are an author's dream come true!

And to all my family and friends who have always supported me.

Contents

PART FOUR
Q&A with an Ex-Con

Preface

Panty Hose and a Pistol

It is not important how we come to the events in our life.
What is important is how we deal with those events.

—TROY EVANS

PANTY HOSE AND A pistol. I am sure that neither the Hanes Corporation nor Smith & Wesson ever intended for the two to be used within the same sentence, or together in the title of this book's preface. As a former bank robber, however, these were the tools of my trade. As a professional speaker, they continue to be today.

When delivering a presentation on making life changes, I start by thanking the audience for their time and letting them know that it is both my pleasure and my honor to be there with them to share my story. I then ask them to take a close look at my face. I explain that this is the face of a loving father. This is the face of a college graduate who earned both of his degrees with the highest academic honors. This is the face of a kind man, an honest man, a trustworthy man: a man of his word. For humor, I throw in that this just may be the face of a man who could sit them down at their kitchen table and sell them a term life insurance policy. As the chuckles die down, I again ask them to take a close look at this face. I then turn my back to the audience, pull panty hose over my head and turn back around while leveling a replica of a semiautomatic pistol in their direction. I then ask them to take a look at my face again. This is the face of a man who, on March 20, 1992, walked into the First Tier National Bank, pointed a semiautomatic pistol at the face of the teller, and demanded all of the twenties, fifties, and hundreds—my first of five armed bank robberies committed during a six-month crime spree. Once more, I ask them to please take a close look at my face.

In my life, I have worn both faces. The transformation between the two—from suicidal, drug-addicted bank robber to what I am today—took place gradually over seven and a half years within the confines of a federal prison. I use this opening because it grabs my audience by the throat. Surely the clean-cut, suit-sporting, accountant-like man standing before them would be more likely to pull out a flip chart than a deadly weapon, right? After all, my introduction paints a picture of an all-American boy whose academic credentials have placed him on both the Dean's and President's Lists. But I do it because I need their attention. I do it because, if I can meet every set of eyes while I am telling my story, if every person whose eyes I meet listens to my story, not a single person in the room will leave unchanged.

In Roman mythology, there is a god with two faces named Janus. He is the god of gates and the god of beginnings and is depicted with two faces so that he can look both forward and backward at once. I think about him often because my story involves the two faces of my past and my future. It is a story of creating new beginnings and a story of passing through a gate; representative of both the cold, real prison bars that I was behind for a large portion of my life and the threshold I crossed when I left my past behind and chose my future. As you read this book, I want you to remember Janus.

Who are you now? Who do you want to be? What has kept you from being the person that you want to be? I believe that human beings can adapt to any type of adversity and I believe that we all have room to make positive changes in our lives. This book is for those of you who are standing at the gate of your new beginning, looking at the past and preparing to choose a future as the person who you want to be. It is my hope that you can learn from my story, that I can help you to embrace change and take that first step.

Am I proud of the fact that I went to prison? Absolutely not. Do I feel remorse for my victims, and for the pain and shame that was borne by my family? Every day of my life. But am I proud of the fact that I took a desperate situation and turned it into the life I lead? Definitely. Do I believe that my struggles, accomplishments, and life lessons can benefit everyday people in everyday lives? Absolutely.

That is why I wrote this book and that is why I spread my message and story to as many people as possible. Over the next twenty chapters as I share my story with you—my ups and downs, good times and bad times—I ask that you read my words not as coming from a bank robber turned speaker, but as coming from a man telling you that the only thing that can truly hold you back in life is you.

PART ONE

What Was I Thinking?

If you have made mistakes, even serious ones, there is always another chance for you. What we call failure is not the falling down but the staying down.

—Mary Pickford

Chapter 1

From Cub Scout to Con

Everything you have in your life is there because you attracted it.

—MIKE WICKETT

WE ALL MADE CHOICES to get where we are today. If we stand at the gate of change and look back, some of us can pinpoint an exact moment when things started to go wrong. For others, that moment may be blurred, and all we know is that we have spun out of control ever since. For me, it was a little of both.

How did I come to the point of robbing banks? How did I arrive at a time in my life where I was willing to point a gun in someone's face and demand money? I can assure you that I did not aspire to become a bank robber growing up. I did not walk into kindergarten career day and say, "When I grow up, I want to spend a large chunk of my life in prison and cause my family a great deal of pain." That was, however, the path that I chose.

Believe it or not, I was once an honor-roll student. I played baseball and football so well that, even when I was very young, my coaches and parents thought I might go pro one day. I was surrounded by teammates, friends, and coaches who encouraged me to pursue my ambition—to become a professional ball player.

Then, when I was fourteen years old, we moved in the early summer to an entirely different city in an entirely different state, and everything changed. If you've ever moved, you may already be familiar with some of the dynamics of making new friends. There is an initiation process. To get in with the cool kids, you have to show them that you're cool. To get in with the jocks, you have to be a good athlete. But to get in with the "bad kids," all you have to do is be bad. And that's easy to do. Had I been able to join up with a baseball or football team as soon as I moved, I might never have had to make a choice about who I was going to be. But without that as an option, my choices were to wait until the school year and sports seasons began or to make friends immediately with the kids who were most readily available to me—the "bad kids." I made a choice. The easy one.

•

When my family arrived in Colorado Springs in the summer of 1978, I was used to having the whole world laid out for me. I had been born with the gifts of intelligence, coordination, and athleticism. These were the things that defined who I was. I was the "smart kid," the "star of the team." My family status was a given as well. My father was a senior executive for a large organization; we were firmly in the upper middle class. At the age of fourteen, I was too young to understand that these things—the things that had been mine for as long as I could remember—could be taken or, as you'll see, given away.

Until then, I had spent the entirety of my life in Phoenix, Arizona. Residents are blessed with an average of 325 days of sunshine every year. To many of the young boys living in that state, that translates into precisely one thing—a baseball utopia. Baseball is a year-round event in Phoenix and for many of us who played ball together those days are the best memories of our childhood. My memories of it are still as clear as if it were yesterday. By junior high, I was already a star, getting city-wide press and standing out among the best of the best. Those were the days that defined me in my younger years and when I picture my childhood, those are the days that I prefer to linger upon.

My father was a top-level employee at Motorola then. I remember him being very busy, but he would still find time to make it to my games. I remember him talking to our relatives and the other parents at the game and I remember the look of pride that was on his face when he talked about me.

I was the oldest of three and each night the family would come home from work, school, or play, sit around the dinner table, and discuss the day's events. I was often one of the first to speak, telling my dad about the play that I had made that day on the baseball diamond or how I had aced a test. The picture I have in my mind of those evenings is nothing less than Cleaver-family perfect.

One evening, our normally cheerful family dinner was interrupted by my father's latest news. He had been offered a job as a high-level executive in Colorado Springs. We were going to move—away from my friends, away from my school, away from the coaches and recruiters who already knew that I was going to be a star—to a place where my sunshine and year-round baseball season would be replaced with an average forty-three inches of snowfall per year.

We were not asked. Not moving was never even an option. My father had made a decision that affected every single one of us. On paper it looked great. He was going to make much more money and get a high-level executive title. Sure he would have to work longer hours, uproot the family, and start traveling several weeks out of the year, but those are the sacrifices that a man has to make to give his family a better life. Right?

Frankly, I didn't care how it looked, on paper or otherwise. I was not happy.

Even in the best scenarios, change is difficult on kids. At that age, you haven't been around enough to learn to adapt. (Frankly, I know some adults who have a great deal of trouble with it.) I had absolutely no reference point that would tell me that things were going to be okay. What I did have was a list of unknowns a mile long.

When we packed up our things and said our farewells to Phoenix, I could only make uneducated guesses about what to expect from my new home. I wasn't even sure how it could be our "home." All of the ideas I had surrounding that word could not possibly be associated with this new place. It was not familiar. It was not comforting to me. It did not feel like a safe haven. It felt lonely and isolating. Colorado Springs made me feel like I simultaneously stood out and was invisible. I wasn't a local, so people noticed me for being new, but that didn't mean they were rushing to greet me. Many of them seemed to stand back and wait to see where I would fall into the high-school pecking order.

It was the summer, so there was no school, there was no baseball, and my dinner conversation topics were fairly scant. Of course, dinner itself had been altered anyway, since my father's new job required that he travel very often. It seemed as though he was gone as often as he was there while he adapted to the requirements of his new job, and we were left to try to make a home out of the new house with the strangely quiet dinner table.

I decided that the best thing to do would be to make friends with somebody, anybody, just so I wouldn't be alone. That would make everything better. I wouldn't be lonely and I wouldn't stand out quite so much.

At fourteen, I wasn't old enough to drive yet, so my entertainment was limited to the friends and activities that I could find within walking or biking distance of my house. As it turns out, I didn't have to go far.

Right there, a few blocks away, was the perfect group for the new kid in town. There were no requirements for being their friend. I didn't have to prove myself at tryouts, as I would have had to do with the jocks. I didn't have to show that I was cuter, funnier, or better at bullying nerds, as I would have had to with the cool kids. These were the "bad" kids. All I had to do to hang with them was be bad. Sure, I had moments of conscience that told me that I wasn't supposed to be smoking a joint or stealing money from my mom's purse, but they were quickly overcome by the feelings of excitement over not getting caught and relief at having made friends in a new town. I was not going to be an outcast, as I had feared. I had found a group.

Even better, at the center of that group, shining like a beacon to my newly relocated soul, was the girl of my dreams. I was drawn to her with all of the force that can be mustered by the raging hormones of a fourteen-year-old boy. If she smoked pot, I sure as heck was going to as well. Even better, she helped me let go of some of my reservations because she was an athlete, too. If she could live in both worlds, so could I.

In my mind, I had it made. I would be able to enter school without too much harassment for being the "new kid," and I was enjoying the thrill of being the "bad kid." I had a girlfriend and the discovery of marijuana to make my life more exotic, and I wouldn't have to give up the "good kid/star of the team" persona that I had held to that date. There was no downside!

Let me pause in the story here to say that there is nothing more dangerous than the fourteen-year-old mind. Based on the minutiae of information I had accumulated in my short life, I was fantastic. Truly, that was my identity: I was fantastic. My parents, teachers, and coaches had always told me so. I was also bulletproof. Gifts and talents were not things that could be lost. My parents' adoration and faith in me were absolutes. I was entitled to these things. I didn't have to worry about drugs. My friends, and more importantly, my wonderful, beautiful girlfriend, told me so.

That's why it was so hard to understand when it all began to unravel.

I started sneaking out at night to hang with the group, screw around with my girlfriend, and smoke some weed. I needed to finance the pot and subsequent munchies, so I started taking money from my mom's wallet or absconding with various objects around the house. I was absolutely sure that they would never notice. After all, parents are dumb, right?

To my fourteen-year-old amazement, my parents weren't so dumb after all. It didn't take long before they stopped looking at me like I was the golden child and started questioning my every move.

Our strangely quiet dinner table was now filled with a new kind of daily recap.

As I said, my dad was out of town a lot of the time. My mother tried to keep me home, but at that point I was bigger than she was. What was she going to do?

She did the only thing she could. She said, "You wait until your father gets home," and then gave him a call.

By the time the old man did get home, he was often so mad from the stories that he had heard during the week that he was ready to nail me the instant he set foot through the door. While I did have a healthy fear of my father's ability to drive the point home, I also already had the cunning of an addict able to manipulate my mother's love at will.

My father had been raised to be a heavy-handed disciplinarian. His theory on parenting prescribed swift, harsh punishments that would drive the point home. If I were going to act like a loser, he was going to treat me like one, so that there would be no question as to the cause and effect of my actions.

My mother, on the other hand, like many mothers who find themselves in similar situations, was still unable to let go of the image of the sweet boy that I had been. After all, it was just months ago that I had been that child. She could only hold out hope that this was a temporary phase. That, coupled with her fear that too harsh a punishment would drive me away for good, was all I needed.

I fed my mother's delusion like I fed my own habit. Why shouldn't I? It's not like I was really in trouble, right? They were dumb rules anyway.

I wasn't a baby. I didn't need a curfew. And what were a few bucks borrowed here or there? They could afford it.

To top it off, I was so mad at my dad for having moved us away from our home that I figured he got what he deserved. From what I knew, people didn't get addicted to pot, so there was no fear in my mind that I was in any actual danger. Like I said, I was bulletproof. But my dad, on the other hand, had to deal with the neighbors knowing that his kid was doing drugs. He was getting phone calls at work from my mother and my little pastime was making his life downright uncomfortable. That was all the incentive I needed to justify it in my mind. I'd show him. That job wasn't looking so good now, was it?

Inevitably, my father would come home, wound up from having to deal with his delinquent son and the stresses of a new job, and my mother would begin intervening on my behalf almost instantly. It's amazing that their marriage stood up to it. He would try to ground me and she would let it slide during the week when he was out of town. He would try to lock me out at night and she would make him let me back in. Life at home was no holiday, but that just gave me yet another reason to stay away more often and do some more drugs. And, frankly, they were so distracted by arguing over what was going to happen to me that I could generally slip out during the fray practically unnoticed.

Of course, the summer couldn't last forever and soon I was back to school, ready to resume my status as the family star in my new double life. Surely the folks would ease up a bit with a new stream of A's and the beginning of the sports seasons.

I soon found out, however, that my two lives were not as compatible as I'd believed. I discovered, much to my shock, that it's incredibly hard to balance a habit and the responsibilities of everyday life. By then I had graduated to smoking pot every day and was even starting to experiment with some of the harder stuff. It made it very hard to concentrate on school—that is, when I wasn't skipping it to get high.

It did kind of hit my radar that those A's weren't rolling in like I had expected. Fortunately, I had the benefit of drugs to help relieve my conscience of any clarity that might have interceded at this point. The drugs had already taken over and I was starting to lead a not-so-double life, with this new, addicted me playing the lead role.

My teachers were giving me C's and D's and the principal was constantly riding me about absences. What they didn't understand, or maybe did but had no way to combat, is that my friends actually encouraged me to perform this way. I was getting all of the positive reinforcement I needed from my wonderful support group, and I didn't mind the failing. I thought, *I could get A's if I tried. I don't need to jump through hoops for these people.*

Unfortunately, "these people" also included my coaches. At any given time, I was in danger of becoming ineligible to play because of my grades. Not that I was playing much anyway. Suddenly, the things that had come so easily to me before—pitching, fielding, hitting—were hard to do. In junior high, I had scouts from junior colleges looking at me. The expectation was that high school would bring the college and university scouts. But that wasn't the case. Thanks to the drugs, I no longer had the coordination or the stamina. Instead, my coaches said things like, "We were told great things about you, that you were going to go pro someday, and we're wondering why." I was getting benched and baseball wasn't fun anymore.

I had all kinds of empirical evidence that drugs were doing me harm, but my young brain just couldn't make sense of it. Drugs weren't supposed to do this to me. My girlfriend was able to straddle both worlds; why couldn't I?

When I couldn't make sense of it, I let the paranoia flow in. The beautiful thing about paranoia is that it absolves you of blame. It's always *someone else* who's out to get you. Once it's out of your hands, there's no use trying to fight the tides. You might as well just accept it.

Paranoid justification in action:

- *My grades are dropping because these teachers have it in for me. Who cares? It was never cool to be the "smart kid" anyway.*
- *I would have been able to make that catch if the coaches were giving me enough play time. If they can't realize how great I am, then I don't want to play for them anyway.*

Baseball was, of course, the toughest thing to let go of. I really had wanted to be a professional athlete. Not long into the season, however, the choice was made for me. I was cut from the team. It took me two weeks to admit it to my family.

Looking back, that was the best opportunity that I had to get myself out of trouble. There was no hiding the issue at that point and drugs had finally cost me something that I had truly wanted. Of course, the only people who were giving me guidance at that point were my "friends."

Talking to my parents was out of the question because we were all too busy yelling at each other. The coaches had given me all the chances that they could. It wouldn't have been fair to the other players to cut me any more slack. In the end, it came down to me and the other guys, smoking a little pot, and deciding that the coaches had it in for me from day one, so I'd be dumb to play for that team anyway.

Amazingly, when I finally did tell my parents that I had been cut, it was like sweet surrender. I was actually relieved. I had been balancing two lives for so long that I didn't want the pressure anymore. It would have been nearly impossible to put my life back the way it was before I started using drugs. My parents didn't trust me and I didn't think they would any time soon, even if I turned it around. It was too late for school and sports. Why bother hanging on to that side of myself anymore? It was just easier to let it go and put all of my efforts into my new identity—Troy Evans, drug user.

My addiction had started out as casual marijuana use, just occasionally on the weekends, but it had grown quickly. Before I knew it, and it seemed like overnight, drugs had become the most important thing in my life. Within the span of two years, my life degraded so much that soon every event, intention, and action had to do with acquiring and using drugs. There was not a single aspect of my life that was not affected by drug use. At this point, I was so far gone that I wasn't even welcome at the family dinner table anymore. My name brought nothing but misery, pain, and anger to the conversations.

I eked my way out of high school with C's and D's and immediately turned to the only profession that could feed my habit and pay the bills at the same time: I dealt drugs. It was obvious that this was the only occupation that would allow me to support a habit that had now grown to the point of daily use of nearly every hard drug available on the streets.

At this point, I was climbing further and further out on a limb. Some of my "bad" friends began to see the error of their ways and pull back. Others were able to keep their impulses in check and function in society. Not me. My whole world was now about one thing only—staying high.

My parents—especially my mother—still held out hope. They tried tough love, letting me run free to see if I could get the wildness "out of my system," getting me into rehab (three thirty-day stints, none of which made a damn bit of difference) at considerable expense. If not for my mother, my dad probably would have killed me, or at the very least thrown me out on the street. He'd had enough of my stealing from him and other family members, not to mention the disgrace I brought upon the family.

After high school, I finally moved out, working at a string of meaningless jobs that were a screen for my activities as a drug dealer and my main desire—to party all the time.

Two years out of high school, I met a girl and got her pregnant. In a truly awkward attempt at being the responsible person I'd been before the drug days, I married her. Our son was born a few short months later. Bringing a child into this world is supposed to be a beautiful thing. Bringing Eric into this world was not. I would look into his crib knowing that I had just helped create a new life, a new person whom I knew I would hurt somehow. And so I did. I later abandoned him, and he became yet another person on the long list of those who were devastated by my drug addiction. Bringing my son into this world should have been the most beautiful event in my life. With my addiction tucked firmly at the top of my priority list, it wasn't. I made a choice. I could have chosen my family . . . my son . . . sobriety. I chose drugs. It was easier.

After four years of putting up with my lying, cheating, drug-addicted ways, my wife filed for divorce and won primary custody of my son. I didn't think that there was more downhill still available in my life, but I quickly discovered that the gutter has amazing depth.

I chose to leave the small town where my son and ex-wife resided, but I found I had nowhere to go. My addiction had now reached the point where I literally could not hold any type of job. Not only did a position not exist which could support my daily intake, but I had also reached the point where I stayed so high throughout the day—on meth, cocaine, heroin, prescription drugs, crack, alcohol, and anything else I could get my hands on—that I could not perform even the simplest of tasks. It was at this point, when I had zero ability to hold a job or maintain a residence, that I turned to robbing banks.

Picture my situation: By this time, I had burned every bridge I'd ever built with family and friends. I couldn't stay with them, so I'd move from seedy hotel to seedy hotel, sleeping on the streets when I didn't have enough money to pay for a room. When I began robbing banks, I was beyond desperate. I figured I would come out of the bank with enough money to feed my habit for another thirty to sixty days—or the police would confront me, I would brandish my gun, and they would put me out of my misery. It's called "suicide by cop." I wanted the police to do something I did not have the courage to do myself.

Bank robbery, incidentally, is not glamorous or anything like the well-planned heists often portrayed by Hollywood. Most bank robbers are like I was at the time—acting out of desperation and with nothing to lose. The majorities are strung out on drugs, or have a gambling debt to pay, or have a house that is about to be foreclosed on; in short, they've reached the end of their rope.

That's where I was—at the end of the line. To me, robbing banks was a no-brainer. It was a win-win situation. Bank tellers, unlike convenience store clerks, are unlikely to pull a gun out from under the counter, making it one of the safer jobs I could pull. Either I came out of that bank with enough money to feed my addiction, or the police showed up and I would force a confrontation that would take my life.

I'm not going to tell you that my decision to rob banks came without any difficulty. There remained a small part of me that realized that what I was doing was very wrong. There were at least a dozen banks that I entered, gun in waistband, intent on completing the job, only to hand the teller a $10 bill while requesting a roll of quarters. But what was the alternative? Confronting my life, acknowledging the person I had become and the things I had done along that road, while going through withdrawals? That did not even seem to be an option.

There was no going back. I had made so many bad decisions that finding a path to a better life had grown into a monumental feat in my mind. It was just too hard. So I took the easy path instead—drugs or death. Either way, I figured it would soon be over. It was far easier to take a hit and live my life within the sweet release of apathy.

Then the unexpected happened. Rather than overdosing or getting myself killed, I was caught. I had already committed five robberies at that point and the police had no clue I was the perp. In a last-ditch effort to nab me, the authorities broadcasted information about the robberies in the newspaper and on local news shows. An ex-girlfriend, who was no fan of mine, saw me with a large sum of money and put two and two together. We had parted on bad terms, so she had no qualms about calling Crime Stoppers on a hunch.

She told them where I was staying, another low-rent hotel. The police called the room, pretending to be management. It was early morning, and they knew I had a gun, so their goal was to get me to come out of the room without it. The voice on the phone said that if I were staying another night, I had to come pay for it immediately. When I did not respond to the first call, they called again. I got up and, completely oblivious, started toward the office wearing just flip-flops and shorts. Halfway there, I realized something was going on. The next thing I knew, there were a dozen guns drawn on me. I had no opportunity to point a gun at them, which meant my plan had failed. They weren't going to end my miserable existence for me.

There I was, face on the ground, knee in my back, cuffs on my wrists, facing the horror of what lay ahead of me. The drugs didn't get me. I wasn't cut down in a reign of bullets. I was being loaded into the back of a police car, with my shorts, flip-flops, and no idea what was to come.

At the time, naturally, I was not happy with my ex-girlfriend. But in retrospect, she literally saved my life. I have no doubt whatsoever that I would have died on the path I was on. That was, after all, the plan.

As it was, my life was about to become a thousand times more difficult than it had been on the easy path to destruction. I was convicted of robbing banks and sentenced to thirteen years in the federal prison system.

•

Some say you should forget about your past and concentrate on your future, but for those who are looking to make a change, that is tantamount to sticking your head in the sand. As they say, those who forget about history are bound to repeat it.

I am often asked about my childhood entry into the world of drugs. I can't give a speech without parents coming up to me at the end, with the look that I've come to know too well, asking me how I started using drugs and what they should do to prevent their children from becoming addicts. I look at the pain in their faces and I can remember glimpses of the same look that, on the rarest of occasions, managed to make it through my own drug haze years ago—the look of my parents desperately trying to hang on to the child who they loved.

I last saw it the final time I was invited to a family Christmas. It was rare that I made it to a family event after high school, and the majority of my relatives were relieved when I didn't show up. My mother was the last to hold on to hope.

I repaid her hope by showing up to Christmas dinner too stoned to function. I spent the entire holiday party passed out on my parents' bed. When I finally came to and reappeared, it was to see that my mother no longer had the look of pain or hope that had always told me that I was still her little boy. She had a quiet resignation that told me that I was never going to ruin a family get-together again. I was no longer welcome.

That is just one of the memories that continues to haunt me today. It is painful every time I think about it, but it is important that I don't forget it. I think that in order to move forward, we must first recognize where we come from. That means confronting wrongs and accepting responsibility. To become the man that I am today, I first had to acknowledge and take responsibility for that memory and the numerous other wrongs that I had perpetrated against family, friends, and perfect strangers alike. Even in a drug-induced haze, I knew that the process would be painful. That pain, more than anything else, was what kept me from making the changes that I needed to make. It made me fool myself, point fingers, contrive excuses, and it had me locked inside a prison long before I was behind bars. But I needed to acknowledge my past and accept responsibility before I could ever move forward. I had to forgo the easy path and truly face what I had become and the things I had done.

Have you ever wondered why they make addicts introduce themselves at meetings as addicts? "Hi, my name is Troy and I'm a drug addict." It's because if we say our secret out loud, it's not a secret. And if it's not a secret, we have to deal with it.

Drug addicts are great con artists. It's an important part of the addiction because, in addition to fooling our friends and family, we have to fool ourselves. We tell ourselves we're fine, we don't need any help, it's not affecting our work, it's not affecting our families, and we do it because the truth is too terrible.

My first wife brought my family together for an intervention once. I came home to a room full of family, friends, co-workers, and my boss. For every excuse that I gave, they had a reply.

"I can't go to rehab now. I have to work."

"That's okay, Troy, you can have the time off," replied my boss.

"I have to be here to tend to the livestock."

"That's okay," said my neighbors. "We'll pitch in and help."

"I don't have anything packed."

"I've packed a bag for you," said my wife and, after several more attempts at excuses that they had already thought of, off we went.

They prepare families of drug addicts to cover all of the bases like that, because addicts always have excuses. We have them because saying "I have to work" sounds rational and responsible, whereas the alternative, the truth that is screaming through our heads, is just too awful to say aloud. I mean, how could anyone, drug addict included, look his family in the eye, look at himself in the mirror, and say the truth: "I can't go to rehab until I've had one more hit. I choose drugs over you, me, everyone, and everything. I am willing to steal from you, jeopardize your safety, and leave you without your son, husband, father in exchange for my next hit."

Someone recently asked me why, when I was making all of those pivotal decisions in my life, I couldn't just take the mask of the bank robber off or stop using drugs. Back then, while I was living in the world of drugs and crime, I had dozens of excuses. Looking back now from my life as a clean, law-abiding citizen, however, I realize that the question shouldn't be "Why couldn't I?" but rather "Why didn't I?" It was never a question of can or can't. I'm proof today that I could have all along. The simple answer is that I chose not to.

To quit, I would have had to admit I was addicted. To admit I was addicted would mean that I had to look at my actions as an addict. To look at my actions would have been too horrible for me to bear. To become the man I wanted to be, I had to let my secret out. I had to acknowledge the person I had been, and I had to claim the pain that I had caused everyone. I had to confront my past and claim responsibility.

We live in a society of victims. You can't turn on the news without someone telling you why he or she is a victim. It is only on the very rarest of occasions that reporters are able to tell us of someone who refused to take that role and, instead, chose to make a difference in his or her own life.

Maybe you're battling an addiction like I was. Or maybe the thing you want to change most about yourself is your weight, job, or education. Whatever it is, in order to claim your past you have to take away all justifications for your current situation and tell yourself that you aren't satisfied with your status going forward.

If I throw my hands up and say that I was a drug addict and bank robber because I was a victim of a family move when I was a teenager and lost my support network, there will always be people there to pat me on the back and say, "Poor Troy." But it will never help me get better, because you can't improve yourself by giving your power away. I have to own my decisions. If I claim them, no matter how bad they are, I claim the power that I have always had to control my destiny and to make the changes that I want to make in my life.

That is the first and hardest step of them all—putting down the excuses and taking absolute responsibility for who you have been up to this point and what happens to you as you move forward.

Chapter 2

Juvenile Injustice

The person who sees what he wants to see, regardless of what appears, will some day experience in the outer what he has so faithfully seen within.

—ERNEST HOLMES

FOR EVERY CHANGE, THERE is one pivotal point—a point where the status quo is abandoned and an entirely new direction is chosen. The laws of physics state that objects in motion tend to stay in motion. To stop or redirect that object takes effort. This applies to life changes as well. Reversing a trend that you have spent a lifetime building can take a great deal of power, but sometimes great power is wrapped in very small packages.

May 7, 1993. It proved to be the hardest day I had ever faced. That was the day I stood before a federal judge and was told that I would spend the next thirteen years in federal prison. The next 157 months of my life were going to be spent as an incarcerated felon. To that date, it was the hardest day of my life...but it was nothing compared to the next.

May 8, 1993. That was the day I had to call my then seven-year-old son Eric and let him know his dad was not going to be available to him for a very long time. "Incarceration" is a hard enough concept for an adult to fathom. For a seven-year-old child, a third grader, it's impossible. Eric could not even comprehend the span of thirteen years. How do you understand an amount of time almost twice your own age? All he wanted to know was whether he was going to be able to come spend next summer vacation with me, as had been the case the prior three years.

"No, Eric, you won't be coming to spend next summer vacation with me."

"Well, how about the one after that, Dad?"

"No, Eric, not that one either."

"Well, for sure the one after that, right, Dad?"

"No, Eric, not the one after that either."

After asking a few more times, he finally asked, "When do I get to come spend the summer with you, Dad?"

"Maybe the one when you turn eighteen, Eric. That will be the next time you get to spend a summer vacation with your daddy."

I said in the last chapter that in order to change, I had to come clean with my worst secrets, so let me share a few of those with you right now.

The day my wife went into labor, I called my friends with the good news. That was their cue to gather up a bunch of booze and cocaine and assemble a little tailgating party in the hospital parking lot.

For the next eight hours, I ran non-stop between delivery room and the impromptu parking lot drug party, creating an absolute, drug-induced haze around what should have been the most significant day of my life.

At one point, I entered my wife's delivery room to see an entire team of doctors and nurses attempting to reach my son's head in the birth canal with a probe because there were some extreme complications. I was so hopped up that I couldn't even comprehend what was going on. I watched the scene for as long as I could stand it and then returned to the parking lot. I didn't know what was happening, but I knew I needed a hit to help me get through whatever was going on.

Fast forward to when my son was a young boy, just four or five years old. By this time, his mother and I had separated and he would come and visit me for the summer. There I was, the pillar of fatherhood, stoned out of my mind and supporting my habit by dealing drugs. Our summers were filled with adventures like tubing down the Salt River with my closest addict friends, while we drank ourselves silly and then capped it off with a drunken race down the Beeline highway on our way home.

On an average day, I would try to steer him away from my drug stashes and take him shopping in true Disneyland Dad fashion. My boy had the best stuff that drug money could buy. I didn't worry about making him brush his teeth, bathe, follow rules or any of the other things that I should have done as a father, but I did revel in the fact that each fall, I would return an absolute monster to his mother, one who talked non-stop about how great it was at his dad's.

While parenting is supposed to be a full-time job, I figured that really only meant daylight hours. After all, how much parenting do you really have to do at night? He's asleep anyway. So at bedtime, I would tuck him into bed, often in some seedy hotel room, and then take off for hours to go party. That's right. I would literally leave a small child alone in a room, usually in a neighborhood where grown adults wouldn't feel safe, because the drugs were just more important. In fact, I thought I was doing the responsible thing. It wasn't like you could just bring a small child to a party with drugs, right? That would be crazy.

As if that weren't enough, here's the one that earned me the Father of the Year award. One summer while Eric was visiting, I dropped him off at a friend's because I had to go and "run an errand." Then I went and robbed a bank.

If something had happened to me during the robbery, nobody would have even known where to find him. He was cooped up with one of my drug buddies for a babysitter.

Then of course there is the fact that I eventually got pinched for bank robbery and was sent to prison.

When my son was fortunate enough to be out of my care, he lived in a very small Midwestern town. *Everybody* knew his business. *Everybody* knew where his daddy was. *Everybody* knew his dad was a convict. Kids can be extremely cruel, and I knew that what I had done would cause my son to be teased, tormented, and ridiculed for years to come. I had let him down throughout his life and going to prison was going to make it even worse. I dreaded the question that I knew would always hang in his eyes, the "Why?" that I would never be able to answer. The first time I saw Eric in the prison visiting room, however, I came around the corner to hear my son asking a guard a very different question. "If you won't let my dad spend the night with me at the hotel tonight, can I spend the night in here with him?"

It hit me like a ton of bricks. Despite everything my son had just gone through he still wanted to stay the night here with me in prison. Despite all of the slamming steel doors behind him, despite having to take off his belt and shoes while going through a metal detector, and despite, at seven years old, being "patted down" to see that he wasn't smuggling in contraband, I was still a hero in his eyes. I was still his Daddy no matter where I was and what I did. On that day when he visited, I went from being a nameless, faceless convict among 1,200 inmates—Evans #24291-013—to being a hero. I wanted to grab him, squeeze him, and say thank you for still loving me!

That day I came to two very important realizations. Number one, drugs had become more important to me than the most important person in my life. It really had become that simple—drugs meant more to me than my son did. And, number two, I was breaking a long-standing tradition. The tradition of my great-grandfather being there for my grandfather, my grandfather being there for my dad, and my dad being there for me.

My father's role in my life was a stark contrast to mine in my own son's. When my father was eighteen, he married my mother and worked full-time while going to school full-time. He was incredibly successful, but always made time to make it to my baseball games. Our weekends and summers were filled with hunting, fishing, and camping. He taught me that men held their word dear, worked hard, didn't lie, didn't cheat, and didn't steal. That information was passed down through generations of men in my family. I broke that chain.

Did I ever once take my son hunting or fishing? Not a chance. Where would I get drugs in the woods? Did I ever show him how to sharpen a knife, stop game, spot birds? That's pure insanity. I couldn't even focus most of the time.

Instead of being there for my son, I gave him an absent father, ridicule at school, and the eternal question that was always on the tip of his tongue no matter how cheerful he tried to be: "Why did you leave me?"

Incarceration, detention, and prison—they all mean the same thing. They are deprivation. My son had been deprived of his father for all seven years of his life, and I was looking with fear at a thirteen-year prison sentence having never realized that my son had been born into a prison of his own, and his only crime was being born to a father who had made drugs his priority. And yet I heard him asking again and again if he could be with me. I heard the hope in his voice for a father who had never even been very good at being one, and I decided right then and there that I was going to be a better man. Steel bars or no, I was going to be as close to the father that my son deserved as I could possibly be. If my son still had hope for me, then I could have hope as well.

That was it. That was my pivotal point.

•

Like I said before, sometimes the power that you need comes in small packages. For me, it was the hope of a child. Great things can be learned from children.

Remember when you were a child? Didn't you believe that you could be anything you wanted when you grew up? Somewhere along the line, we stop believing that. We lose hope that our life has the potential to be anything else but what it already is.

I saw hope for my future reflected in my son's image of me. At the time, I was the least deserving person of my son's hope in the entire world. I knew what I had done to him and yet here he was, looking to at me like I had been the best father on Earth. In that instant, I regained something that I had lost back in the earliest days of my drug use—the hope that there might actually be a way out of the existence I had created for myself; the chance to turn it all around.

Once I caught a glimmer of that hope, I began to see it when I looked at my reflection in the mirror. He taught me that. He taught me to start believing that anything was possible again. He taught me to live my life with the hope of a child.

Suddenly I saw a path ahead of me. I had a vision of the man that I could become, a man that would be worthy of my son's love. What's more, all of the excuses that I had been using to keep myself from changing for all of those years seemed trivial and stupid. I was really going to do it this time. I resolved right then and there that I was going to clean up my act and get rid of the drugs for good. I was going to get the education that I had passed up, be the best dad I could be (even though it meant being the best "prison dad" possible), and I was going to put myself in a position that, when I was finally free to be with my son again, I would be a functioning member of society that he could be proud of.

How many times have you wanted to do something, to make a change in your life, only to get bogged down with all of the reasons why it could never happen? You may say, "I want to go back and get my degree." Then you start to hear a little voice in the back of your head. "How can

I go to class around my work schedule?" "Who will watch the kids?" "I'm too old to go back to school." And suddenly you realize you have been defeated—before you've even picked up a course catalog. I have news for you: it wasn't the job, the kids, or the missed opportunity that defeated you. It was that little voice—the excuses that let you avoid the situation rather than deal with it. They are the same excuses that cover up the real question—"What if I can't?"

I had listened to that little voice all of my life telling me why I couldn't give up drugs, get a job, and love my family. "What if I failed?" "No one would hire me anyway." "My family is better off without me." The little voice was always with me. But the day that I saw hope reflected in my child's face, that little voice started getting fainter and fainter and the possibility of earning the hero status that my son had already bestowed upon me became greater and greater. For the first time in my life, I was truly focused on what was most important and it was all due to a child's hope; not my son's, but the hope that had been reawakened in me.

The day I stopped listening to that little voice, the one filled with all of the doubts, insecurities, and excuses that I had always used as a crutch so that I wouldn't have to make the hard decisions or the smart decisions, was the first day I started to live as the new me.

Chapter 3

Awakened Within the Walls

When one door closes, another opens; but we often look so long and so regretfully at the closed door that we do not see the one which has opened for us.

—ALEXANDER GRAHAM BELL

HOPE IS A POWERFUL THING. It has near-euphoric qualities. But hope alone cannot get you to your goal. That is what I found out during the next few days. The days that I knew I was going to prison but had no idea what to expect.

I had spent the last eight months waiting for sentencing in a federal detention facility while going through the trial process. "Federal detention facility" sounds a lot like prison, but there are a few integral differences.

Within the walls of a federal prison, drugs are more easily obtained than they are on the streets. Heroin overdose is a regular occurrence, bloodshed over drug deals gone bad takes place routinely, and stemming the drug flow into the institution is a constant battle for the staff. I wasn't ready to face that availability on my own. That eight-month period within the detention facility gave me a chance to clear my head, to think rationally, and to make a conscious decision to turn my life around without the persistent stream of drugs that the prison system would have to offer. That was the best and only leg up that the system gave me.

Without the drugs, I gained clarity. With that clarity came some of the scariest moments of my life. I had no idea what to expect when I arrived at my permanent facility. Faced with a thirteen-year prison sentence, I'm sure you can imagine the apprehension and fear that I felt. This was pure, unadulterated reality, no drug haze to stifle the fear. My brain cells were operating at full capacity and, for the first time in years, I knew true fear. My son had given my life value again. In the short period of time I had within the relative safety of the detention facility, I went from being a suicidal drug addict to a man with too much to lose. Now I was facing the legends of prison.

I, like everyone else, had heard stories of the terrors that take place inside prison walls: the beatings, the rapes, and the murders. The funny thing was that it wasn't any one of those things that kept me awake at night. It was all of them and none of them and various combinations. What would it be like? Would it be as Hollywood portrayed it in the movies? Would I be beaten, stabbed, forced into a gang? All I knew was that I wasn't looking forward to fresh-meat orientation and whatever that might have implied. Then it dawned on me. My greatest fear was not simply that I would have to face all of these potential threats, but that if I were to carry through with my promise to my son, and to myself, I would have to do it without the drugs.

During that time, I thought about drugs a lot. I craved the numbness. I wanted that familiar switch that I could flick to make all of my worries go away. For the majority of my life, I hadn't faced a single challenge. I had used drugs to escape them all.

I knew that this was a challenge I needed to face head on if I were going to come out of this the man I wanted to be. So, on the day that I first entered the Florence Federal Correctional Institution, that was the way that I approached it. Head up, with a brave face. Was I scared? You can't begin to imagine. But since then I have learned that the only way to face change is to embrace it, welcome it, and learn to love it with your head up and wearing a brave face.

•

There are of course several dangers within the walls of prison, but one of the greatest perils to a person's soul and the society that inherits that person upon his release is what I call "dead time." It seemed to hang physically in the air, as though it were something you could touch or feel around you. When I first arrived in prison I would sit in the common areas and watch guys play cards, play dominos, and watch TV.

Some of them would spend their entire sentences doing the same thing, for up to sixteen hours a day, day after day, week after week, month after month, year after year, in five-, ten-, fifteen-, even twenty-year stretches. Watching them, I decided that this was not the way I was going to spend the next eleven and a half years of my life. Playing cards and watching talk shows were not going to keep me on my path, and they certainly weren't going to help me pay the bills once I was out. That's when I realized that being inside walls and razor wire was not the prison; dead time was.

While inside, I could see the emptiness in the eyes of my fellow inmates and I knew that dead time was not good enough for me. The irony is that I had been serving my dead time before I ever got to prison. I just never recognized it.

Having spoken to so many people who have had drugs affect their lives personally or through a loved one, my greatest wish is that I could for one moment let every person, every teenager, every potential user, experience what it's like to live the life of a drug addict. It is the epitome of the definition of dead time. I wasn't living my life. I didn't have a chance. Every thought, every resource, every second of my time was spent trying to feed a habit that could not be satisfied.

Whether I ate depended on whether I had money left over after buying my drugs. Even if that was the case, I also had to decide whether it would be worth it to try to keep the food down. I was poisoning my body on a regular basis and even it did not trust me with the things I consumed, food or otherwise.

Whether I worked depended on if I could perform the task while in a drug haze and if there would be sufficient enough breaks throughout the day for me to sneak to the parking lot to stay high. Even if that were the case, it was only a matter of time before I was fired for calling in "sick" too many times, not calling in at all, or because I was so incompetent that they could no longer afford to have me around.

Planning for my future meant looking around in any given instant to see what I had to sell, what there was to steal, which family member still let me into their home. Long-term security meant that I had enough drugs to last me for three days.

I can look back on those days now with clarity and wonder how I ever even survived like that, how I could have chosen that. From a sober standpoint, knowing how bad it was, I can't believe that I chose that dead time day in and day out, and I wish that every child had the benefit of being able to see, with such clarity, the devastation that drugs have on a person.

Of course, as bad as it got, the truth is, the alternative seemed far worse. You have to remember that pulling myself out of the mess I had lived in for a good portion of my adolescence and my entire adulthood meant two things: one, that I would have to face up to what I had done; and two, that I would have to do something I had never done before.

Most of the cons in prison serve the same kind of dead time. Ask them what they did to be sent to prison, and they'll tell you they're innocent. It's better than facing up to what they've done and taking responsibility for it. Ask them what they're going to do that day, and 99.9 percent of the time, it's the same thing they did the day before, and has nothing to do with self-improvement.

Think about your own life. Are you responsible for your situation? What will you do tomorrow that is different from today?

I first noticed my own internal prison by watching my fellow prisoners, but now that I'm on the outside, I see that these prisons have nothing to do with confinement or lack of opportunity. I see people who are perfectly free to take their destinies in hand and create lives of their own choosing instead of choosing dead time, without ever knowing that they are doing it. We sit on our couches, trudge into jobs we don't like, live as people that we don't want to be; we do it day after day, week after week, month after month, year after year. We construct our own prisons, and they are not made of bricks and mortar or razor wire, but of fear of change and the excuses that keep us from confronting that fear.

What is stopping us from having the things that we want? First, we don't want to admit our own culpability in the problem; and second, we fear the change, the "what if."

It's funny, I have to be one of very few people in this world who can make a statement such as this: The very worst thing that ever happened to me in my life, going to prison, is at the same time the very best thing that ever happened to me. There is no doubt in my mind that if I had not been caught, convicted, and incarcerated, I would be dead. There's also no doubt in my mind that if I had not been forced to confront great changes and the overwhelming fear that was associated with them, I could never have become the man I am today. I would never have been awakened from my dead time.

The fear of the unknown keeps us from reaching out, from taking chances, from exploring new possibilities, from pushing ourselves to realize our full potentials. After all, we might not succeed. We might lose our comfort zones. We might *change*! Or, we might succeed. We might benefit. We might be one step closer to actually reaching our goals.

I had help thanks to the officers who arrested me without allowing me to forfeit my life. Only by being forced into the harsh environment of prison was I finally going to make some changes and face my past. Once I did that, I learned that facing change head on and learning to love it made it possible for me to do anything I set my mind to. It is not enough to have hope—that's just the first step. It is the courage to face and embrace change that helps you take the second step. Then what you have is something very powerful—momentum.

Chapter 4

Never Easy

If you want something you have never had, you have to do something you have never done.

—MIKE MURDOCK

MY SON HAD HELPED ME take my first step, and I had found new courage to face my fears and begin building momentum, but then something happened that almost stopped me dead in my tracks—literally.

Since I had been arrested in Denver, Colorado, I was put on trial ninety miles from the brand-new Federal Correctional Complex in Florence, Colorado, the same complex that at one time held Timothy McVeigh and Terry Nichols. Because this new facility was opening up and because they needed bodies, this is where I was sent. And, because I was sent to FCI Florence, I was lucky enough to be situated thirty miles away from home—Colorado Springs. I was just thirty miles from my family and friends, thirty miles from the most important people in my life.

Despite all of my problems, my parents had always been supportive of me in the ways that they could. They had intervened and paid for rehabilitation stays several times, forgiven me for stealing from them on countless occasions, and continued to love me even as I wore away at any faith they could have had left that I would ever do right. But, most importantly, they made the thirty-mile drive and continued to support me while I was going through the roughest years of my life in prison.

This close proximity allowed me frequent visits, almost every week-end. This wasn't the norm. Ninety percent of the inmates I was incarcerated with were from different parts of the country—California, New York, Chicago, Texas, spread throughout the United States. My family's proximity was a blessing to me, but it almost turned into a curse.

Within the federal prison system, gangs run the institutions. As the gangs go, so goes the prison. The Aryan Brotherhood, the Mexican Mafia, the Bloods, the Crips—they dictate what happens behind the walls of many federal prisons. When some of these gang members discovered the frequency of my visits, I was approached by three of them and told that I was going to smuggle drugs into the institution through the visiting room, using my family and my friends as mules, or they were going to kill me.

Each was carrying a shank, which is basically a weapon made out of everyday objects found in a prison, or, as I like to refer to them, the best and brightest products of prison ingenuity. The first guy was carrying a toothbrush. Yes indeed, I said a toothbrush. The difference between this toothbrush and the everyday toothbrush we all use each morning was that an end of this toothbrush had been filed to a very sharp point and the other had been wrapped in duct tape to create a handle. The second guy was carrying a pork chop bone. Once again, you read correctly—a pork chop bone. The long end of the bone had been ground down on the concrete to a very fine point, and the large portion of the bone made a handle that fit nicely in the palm of the hand. This tool is most effective from behind when stuck in the artery of the neck. The third guy was carrying a sixteen-penny nail driven through a six-inch piece of a broom handle. These were the tools by which they would take each others' lives in prison. They were serious. They didn't care that this could mean more time for me, or incarceration for my family and/or friends if we were caught. I was given a choice... if you could call it that.

As they entered my cell and made their demands, I was terrified. My first reaction was that I would do anything they said; I wanted to live. I started to go over my family members in my head to estimate if I had any collateral left with any of them. But as the men gave me their ultimatum and I began picturing the faces of my loved ones, something much stronger than fear came over me. I saw the love that was always there in my parents' eyes, no matter how much I had wronged them. I saw my sister, always ready to stand by her big brother's side. I saw the face of my son and remembered how committed he was to me, regardless of where I was. I thought about the commitment I had made to them to turn my life around, and how it had always been my family that I had sacrificed in the past. I thought about how I wanted to be the person who my son saw me as and who my family was hoping I'd be. And I remembered something that my dad always used to say—a saying I lost track of during my teens and early twenties, but which came back to me in that moment. What my dad used to say was this: "Anything in this life which is really worthwhile, which is *really* worthwhile, is never easy."

Then it struck me. I had been willing to forfeit my life on countless occasions in order to do nothing more than maintain a high. I had been willing to do it every time I walked into a bank, went to buy drugs, or partied to the point where I literally blacked out entire days of my life. That was the easy path. After all, my life had no meaning or worth to me then. Whether it ended by drugs or a bullet didn't matter. If I had been willing to die all of those times for nothing, wasn't it time that I put my life on the line when it actually meant *everything*? Truth be told, was there ever going to be a more appropriate time to make a stand—to save my family, to save my future, to save myself?

All my life I had always taken the easy road. The easy road is the road of drug use. The easy road is a road of lying, cheating, and stealing. Anybody can do these things, it doesn't takes a special type of person; anyone can take the easy road. The more difficult road is a road of self-respect, a road of believing in yourself. It means often standing to one side and feeling alone because it seems that everyone else is heading in a different direction or passing you by, but knowing in your head and in your heart that what you are doing is the right thing.

Peer pressure was the number one driving force in my becoming involved with drugs and heading down the wrong path as a teenager. Everyone wants to be liked; everyone wants to be accepted. It was easier to go along with the pressure than stand alone against it. In prison that pressure is magnified one hundred fold. In prison, not fitting in could cost you your life.

For fourteen years, I had taken the easy road. This was my time to make a stand. I would choose my family over myself. I would choose my integrity over asking my family to bail me out again. I would choose to be true to the goal of becoming the person I wanted to be. I would choose death before I would ever utter the request those men demanded I make.

What happened next? I was saved. The jingle of keys came to us from down the corridor; a guard was on the way. When the gang members heard that jingle, that sweet, wonderful jingle, they took their shanks and tossed them under my mattress. You're only allowed to have two inmates in a cell at any one time, so the guard stuck his head in and said, "Evans, what are these guys doing in your cell?" I told the guard, "They're not doing anything, we're just kickin' it, they're not doing anything at all."

He ordered them out of the cell, and five minutes later I gathered up their shanks and one at a time took them back to their owners, explaining that they had forgotten something. They never bothered me again. Whether it was because I didn't tell the guard what they were doing in my cell that afternoon, or whether it was because they could see in my eyes that I was no longer going to take that easy road no matter what they threatened, they never bothered me again.

I felt like I was rewarded for my decision—as though it was the decision itself that had saved me. I had proven to myself that I was finally ready to put others' lives ahead of my own. But above that, I had chosen myself, as I wanted to be, over the self that I had been. That was no longer good enough for me. Up to that point, I had talked the talk, and now, in one giant stride, a leap of epic proportions when you considered my past, I had taken my first step in walking the walk. I was ready to claim my integrity, stop making excuses, and quit taking advantage of my family's love.

The decision that I made that day in the cell was a momentous victory, but it was a private victory. It was not something I could share with my family. For one thing, I did not want to scare them by recounting it, but more importantly, to tell them that I had made such a significant change in my paradigm would have been lost in the static of a million promises made throughout the years. During my drug use, I had promised my family and myself time and again that I was going to clean up my act. I told them that I had seen the error of my ways, would never hurt them again, and that things would be different. Then, of course, I broke those promises just as soon as I could get my first fix. If there was one thing I knew, it was that I would never win back their faith through words. My words no longer meant a thing to them. I would have to build up a pile of actions twice as high as the mountain of heartbreak I had already delivered, so that my family and friends would be able to draw their own conclusions.

So that's what I did. I never settled for less than absolute integrity from that moment on. I set only the highest goals for myself and accepted nothing less. I etched my word in stone and vowed never to take it lightly again. I was a new Troy, and this one was worth dying for.

My conversion to my new self took on a whole new momentum. I promised to be the model prisoner and make the most of the time I had to spend behind bars. I vowed to be the one prisoner who went an entire year without being written up even once—not for failing to make my bed, not for being late for work. There wasn't a single part of my life, or a single decision made, that wasn't held to absolute scrutiny. At first, it took a conscious effort, but after a while, my new self was more me than my former one. Better yet, every time I chose the harder but right path, the path of integrity, I was rewarded for it. The other prisoners left me alone, the guards gave me a bit more slack, and eventually I became the first, and as far as I know only, prisoner to make it seven and a half years without ever being written up for a single infraction.

I had ventured into the unknown, denounced the easy path for good, and I was rewarded for it.

•

The decision between taking the easy road and staying true to myself was a choice that I had to make daily. I suspect this is the case in many of our lives. The choice is not always as drastic as one between life and death, but is always as simple as choosing an excuse over what you know is right for you. Everyday events are filled with conscious and unconscious decisions and actions that can easily lead us down the easier path. Many people suffer from addictions, abusive relationships, overeating, lack of exercise, overworking. The list goes on and on. These "prisons within ourselves" are just as confining as the steel bars and razor wire that kept me locked up.

When I was addicted to drugs, I was willing to exchange my life at any moment for the prospect of the easy release of a high. While that may seem extreme, many of us forfeit a small part of who we are every day because we are unwilling to look ourselves in the face with the clarity that we deserve. We can imagine the life that we would like to have and make endless promises to try to pursue it, but in the end, we trudge through yet another day without moving toward our goals, choosing the sweet relief of our excuses rather than the more difficult road of action. We hang on to the lies that we tell ourselves and others with a ferocious grip because the alternative means doing something that is new, hard, unknown. If that sounds familiar, you are locked within your own prison, serving dead time just as surely as I was. My sentence was seven and a half years. How long has yours been? How much longer are you willing to settle for it?

In chapter two I talked about finding your pivotal moment. But the truth is, your pivotal moments can come and go in a flash if you do not take action. In chapter three I talked about embracing change, but the reality is that this is much more than just a decision. It is not enough to wake up one morning and say that you are going to change your life forever because the next morning, you may have lost some of your enthusiasm, and your old easy ways will beckon. Changing who you are is not a promise that you make to yourself one day. It is a series of actions that you choose every day for the rest of your life. Some days it will be easy and some days it will be the hardest thing you've ever done. In the end, it is your action that determines how valid your word is and what it means to you.

How many promises have you broken to yourself and others over the years? I am asking you right now to assess what level of integrity you live your everyday life with.

I have the distinct perspective of knowing exactly what it feels like to have no integrity. For years I went through life without a single person, not even my own parents, believing a single word that came out of my mouth. They were absolutely right not to. The advantage I have as I live my life today is in knowing exactly how precious my "word" is, as well as the actions that back it up. Not just my word to others, but also my word to myself.

Have you ever met one of those people who is never on time? (If it's you, pay attention.) These are the people everyone lies to about what time events will start because that's the only way they can get them there on time. They probably think it's a great joke, or maybe they play the constant victim, saying they just can't help it. Do you believe them when they say they will be somewhere on time? Do you feel like you can count on those people when it is truly important?

Many of us go through life breaking our word in little ways through our actions, never really assessing the damage that we are doing to ourselves and those around us. We play fast and loose with responsibility and integrity and never really see the ramifications. Of course, not everyone is like I was in my drug days, cheating and lying to everyone I met. In fact, you may be assuring yourself that you have the highest integrity and you can always be counted on. But I'll ask you this question: Can you count on yourself?

How many times have you said you wanted to change something about your life, made a resolution to do so, and then abandoned it within weeks, days, or even hours because it got hard? If you're like many of us, it has happened more than you care to admit. The problem is that each time we do it, we are reinforcing our own belief that no matter how strong the promises we make to ourselves, we're not going to keep them anyway. Besides, they're just not that important (or at least that's how we excuse it). I can't remember how many times I promised to "try" to kick drugs, never really believing in my heart that I could or would do it.

The fact of the matter is, when you don't back your words and promises up with actions and steel them with absolute determination, they mean nothing. It's not the word but the action that is the key ingredient. You have to go beyond talking the talk and start walking the walk, putting one foot in front of the other no matter how hard the path gets along the way. It's like my dad said: "Anything in this life which is really worthwhile, which is *really* worthwhile, is never easy."

Chapter 5

Power and Responsibility in Prison

The golden opportunity you are seeking is in yourself. It is not in your environment; it is not in luck or chance, or the help of others; it is in yourself alone.

—ORISON SWETT MARDEN

AS I MENTIONED EARLIER, my son drove the first phase of my "awakening." When I discovered that I had the power to influence Eric in a positive direction, it gave me a renewed sense of hope and purpose, a belief that the next several years would be something other than just wasted time, and the feeling that some good could come out of my being imprisoned. For me it would be education. Education was going to be my saving grace.

My child's hope was telling me that I was still the person who had, at one time in life, had a straight-A report card. I remembered how proud I had been to bring home those report cards and how proud my parents had been of me. I remembered a teacher taking me aside when I first started to go downhill and telling me that I was too good for that, and I knew that when I was released, as an ex-con and an ex-drug addict, I was going to need all the help I could get to function in society again. Education would be the means by which I would turn a very negative situation into a positive life change. The bonus was that education was something my son and I could do together. I was excited and ready to get started right away, but I soon learned that I had challenges to face before I could even open my first book.

While some correctional institutions offer work programs, limited vocational programs, and very limited educational opportunities, today's institutions are based more on incarceration than they are on rehabilitation. Federal Pell grants are no longer available to either federal or state inmates, and what meager budgets most institutions are forced to work with are already overburdened with security issues, leaving little or nothing for education or rehabilitation.

I have read studies stating that the recidivism or re-arrest rate of individuals who come out of prison with just two years of college is 10 percent. This compares to a rate of over 60 percent for those who walk out of the prison gates with no education whatsoever. Conservative estimates put costs to incarcerate an individual for a year at $35,000. It would cost a small fraction of that to educate that same individual, and in the long run would prove to be both a savings monetarily and a potentially enormous benefit to society. I could make an argument that we are not doing society a favor by locking up criminals without offering them any rehabilitation, education, or means to rebuild and better themselves. But I can tell you as fact, there was no way I was going to become the man I wanted to be if the only post-incarceration job skills available to me were the ones I could learn from the convicts I was doing time with.

Education was tantamount to the life I wanted to lead. I had made my decision, and I had momentum and determination, but no funding, so I turned to plan B. If Congress wasn't going to give me a chance to improve myself while I was in prison, I would create that window of opportunity for myself.

From the moment I was confronted by the three gang members, I had been living a new life of determination. I was a model prisoner and I had started to stand out among my fellow inmates. For the most part, I was an absolute oddity. At first the guards looked at me with skepticism. They wanted to know why I was being so good. They all knew I was in there for drugs and armed robbery. Surely I was running some sort of a game, and it was just a matter of time before they would find out what I was really up to. But, as I continued my good behavior and continued to improve myself, they started to trust that I was indeed just doing what I said that I was doing: serving my time and trying to be a better man.

To jump-start my education, I started committing every second of my free time to my goal. Every day, every free minute I had, fourteen to sixteen hours a day, day after day, I sat at my tiny little prison desk in my tiny little prison cell, filling out applications, writing essays, begging, pleading, and selling myself to every private scholarship around the country that I even remotely qualified for. These actions received not only the guards' attention, but the prisoners' as well. If the guards didn't know what to make of me, the inmates thought I was downright insane. If you want to know what it's like to go against the grain, try being the object of hundreds of stares of disbelief coming from convicts who can't believe that you're sitting in your cell at a desk, writing away, when the rest of the prison is enjoying special privileges to watch the Super Bowl, the biggest event of the year.

I was breaking the mold, but I had given myself no other choice. I knew that I was a con. I was a felon. No one was waiting in line to take a chance on me. I knew that I would have to convince them and I knew that it was going to be hard, very hard. I got used to reading the words "sorry," "not qualified," "no." Each day at mail call I received a stack of rejection letters... until July 16, 1997.

At that point, I had been incarcerated for four and a half years. I spent those years in a cage and had grown accustomed, as well as one can, to my environment, to the daily disappointments, and to the daily pep talks that would put me back at my desk filling out applications. There was nothing special about this particular day; I was just going about my everyday prison routine when a guard stuck his head in my cell. He informed me that my counselor wanted to see me immediately. I shuffled down the hallway to my counselor's office and was told, "Evans, sit down, I got a phone call on you today from a guy in Auburn, Alabama. He's a scholarship committee chairman, and his association is interested in helping you with your schooling."

I couldn't believe it. I was in shock. I went over the words in my head again. Yes, he had just told me that I had earned a scholarship. The size didn't matter. In spite of all of the wrong paths I had chosen in the past, I had convinced someone, in fact a whole committee of someones, to believe in me.

A week later I received a letter from Robert Henry, the scholarship committee chairman, and a check for one class. The letter informed me that although I did not meet one single criterion specified in qualifying for the scholarship, the committee was so impressed with what I was trying to accomplish that they were going to award me a special stipend.

My first hurdle had been overcome. Then I learned of the second. It was against prison policy for me to receive VHS tapes unless they were pre-screened. The problem was that the lectures for the classes that I was to enroll in were all provided on VHS. I would be required to watch hours of tape and meet prison regulations; every hour would have to be previewed. There was no way the warden would approve man hours to review tape for one con to get his education. This is where I received my second shock.

The counselor at the prison told the warden he was familiar with how hard I had been working to gain an education and that I had been a model prisoner. He said he had heard unbelievable stories from the guards about the prisoner, Evans, who had never caused a single disruption and had never been written up. He said that with the warden's approval, he would be willing to volunteer extra hours before and after work to review my VHS tapes so that I could take the classes.

Up until that point, I had been resolute in waking up each day and believing in myself when no one else would. It was lonely and it was hard. I had been my only cheerleader on a path that only I was certain of, and I was convinced that I was going to have to make the journey alone, noticed only as an oddity. In the course of a few hours, I found out that people who were perfect strangers to me had not only noticed me for the good I was doing, but were willing to take a chance on me. They were willing to put some faith in my ability to turn myself around. It was the first time I had felt that since my early years of high school. It was also the best gift I have ever received. Once again, I was worthy of other people's trust.

I took that one class and sent the association my report card. They then sent me a check for two more classes, and it snowballed from there.

When I landed that first scholarship, Eric took a keen interest in the fact that his dad was going to school. He asked that I send him my graded papers. I think he wanted to see for himself that I was actually going to school like he was. After that Eric showed a renewed interest in his own schooling, and we began to mail our assignments back and forth. He would send me his papers with the little stars, the smiley faces, and the teacher comments. I would send him my test scores, report cards, and term papers, along with the professor comments. It became a competition with us, something that we could do together, something that we could share. As we talked on the phone weekly we would rib each other when one didn't do so well on a test or assignment. My education became a way for me to stay connected with my son, to share something with him, to be a part of his life. I wasn't tossing a baseball back and forth with my boy, but I was doing something with him. You know what I'm saying? I was doing something with my son.

My continuing education and the fact that I was attempting to turn my life around, combined with the positive strides I was making toward becoming a better person, had an effect on others as well. Those on the outside who were following my progress, many of them family and friends who had given up on me long before, suddenly began to ask how I was doing. I was able to start laying a foundation for trust with them again.

My fellow inmates began to notice what I was doing and took an interest. Before I knew it, I had become a prison role model. In fact, the same three inmates who had threatened me with shanks visited me again, but this time, instead of carrying weapons, they came with a request to help them do the same thing I was doing. Those three gang members who rolled in on me, the gang members who came there to take my life if I weren't willing to sling their drugs, now looked to me to save them.

I had turned my life around 180 degrees. I went from a worthless drug addict to a father to my child, a son to my parents, a model of success to a scholarship program, and a role model to my fellow inmates.

I had given myself the best present that I could have received. I used hope to reclaim my self-worth. Then I put my self-worth out to the world until I convinced a scholarship committee to see potential. From potential, I built a full scholarship program and a relationship with my son. From my accomplishments, I taught my parents and loved ones to listen to the hope in their hearts rather than the pessimism of experience. And from there, my worth branched out to people who would never have known who I was, including you reading this book, if I had not believed in myself first.

•

Did you know that Americans have spent billions of dollars on the diet and addiction industries, many of them without any success? The reason for this is that the industries target people who have trouble taking that first step of believing in themselves. In fact, many of the buyers are people who have fallen into a spiral of despair and self-loathing and are using the energy of an infomercial, followed by an impulse purchase, to pull them back out. In the time it takes to read a credit card number over the phone, they can feel better about having taken a first step. The problem is that they are taking the wrong first step.

Take my word for it. Remember, I went to rehab three different times while sliding down the slippery slope toward my own eventual rock bottom. I had taken many first steps, but I never truly had the one ingredient that I needed to make it stick: belief in myself.

Have you ever noticed how hard it can be to take a compliment? Truly genuine compliments have become a rarity in today's society. You may hear niceties spoken daily, such as "nice dress," or "great round" on the course, but when was the last time someone paid you a sincere compliment about your character or your personality? Did you feel awkward receiving it? Did you believe that you deserved it? When was the last time you said something positive to yourself?

When I think back to the moment that I learned of my scholarship money and my counselor's willingness to sacrifice his own personal time to help me in my pursuit of an education, the primary feeling that I can remember is disbelief. It had been so long since I had received positive feedback, I had truly forgotten how to respond. In that moment, it didn't matter whether I had received two new supporters or two thousand. It would have felt exactly the same. Yet had I not believed in myself first, told myself that I could do it—that I had the brains and the determination and the ability to overcome any obstacle that stood in my way—all those letters never would have been written, the scholarship never would have been awarded, and I would not be the man I am today.

The funny thing is that, as hard as it is to take a compliment from a stranger, it is often even harder to take one from yourself. To truly believe that you are capable and worthy of the changes that you want in your life is the greatest gift you can give yourself.

I should never have received my first scholarship check. The organization that sent it to me was the National Speakers Association. The purpose of the scholarship was to fund a college student majoring in speech or communications. As I mentioned before, Robert Henry was the chairman of the scholarship committee at the time. He is the one who convinced the committee to take a chance on a prisoner simply because he was impressed with what I was doing.

After the committee had funded me through a few classes, Robert flew out to Colorado to meet me in person. He told me how impressed he was with me and began writing letters to me weekly. Before long, he was referring to me as his son.

Remember, I had spent the majority of my life with addicts, dealers, and crooks. I had never seen such generosity of spirit. My parents had given up on me long ago and were only just beginning to treat me with guarded optimism rather than resigned disappointment. But Robert had not known me before. He only knew me from what I was trying to do at that point in my life. He was the first person to see the man I was becoming and completely believe it to be true. He could read the commitment in my application and he could see the resolve in my eyes when he came to visit. I believed in myself and was determined to achieve what I had set out to do, and that's what he responded to.

A few years ago, Robert passed away. His secretary and long-time friend called me a few days before he died, and I hopped on the first available plane to be at his side. When I arrived, his secretary told me not to expect a lot. He hadn't spoken a word in three days, and they expected him to pass very soon. As she led me into the room, she said, "Robert, Troy is here." I took his hand, and he turned his head and said, "My third and final son has come. I'm ready now." Then he rolled over and closed his eyes and never uttered another word.

If you asked me when I first met Robert Henry if I would deserve such a gift, I probably would have thought it nearly impossible. At that time, I'm not sure I believed that most of my family, let alone a perfect stranger, would have ever given me that kind of acceptance, faith, and love again. But I'll tell you what I did believe. I believed that from the day I started until the day I took my dying breath, I was going to strive to become the sort of man that could earn it.

If I had never had that level of conviction, if I had never looked myself in the mirror and said nothing short of the best would do, I never would have met Robert Henry. I never would have known the man who I consider to be a second father, and I never would have become the man I am today.

You will never get that gift from anyone but yourself. Who will believe in you if you don't even believe in yourself? It's the old bad news/good news scenario. The bad news is that you are the only one keeping yourself from achieving the things that you want so badly in life. The good news is that you have total control over changing your situation. Believe that, believe in yourself, and you will find that you don't need a first step because you are already running headlong at your goal. The truth is, how you take the first step doesn't matter, so long as you believe in yourself enough to keep walking.

PART TWO

Some Words of Warning

Many of life's failures are men who did not realize how close they were to success when they gave up.

—THOMAS EDISON

Chapter 6

Public Image of an Inmate

A man is not finished when he is defeated; he's finished when he quits.

—RICHARD MILHOUS NIXON

SO I WAS CRUISING ALONG; things were good. I was making my mom and dad proud. I was making my brother and sister proud. I was making my son proud. And I was making my scholarship committee *very* happy. I was two classes away from completing my second degree and already making plans to start on my master's, when a new warden came to FCI Florence. He immediately took a dislike to me. He didn't like the fact that I was allowed extra computer time, he didn't like the fact that I was allowed extra library time, and he particularly did not like the fact that I was allowed to receive videotapes via the mail so that I could take my courses by correspondence. He told me that it was all coming to an end immediately.

I understood that the warden was new and had no way of knowing how hard I had worked to accomplish the things that I had, so I turned to the association that was funding my schooling to plead my case for me. I figured that they had better ground to stand on, not being convicted felons themselves, and they happened to be very well-connected in the political arena.

Over the next several weeks, over two dozen senators and congressmen called and wrote the new warden, demanding to know why I was not being allowed to complete my second degree. Needless to say, he didn't appreciate those calls. In retrospect, I'm sure he felt like his authority was being challenged in his own prison by a convicted felon. He was not used to answering to anyone and now he had his back up against the wall. So he trumped up charges on me, put me under investigation and threw me in the hole, into isolation, as a risk to the institution's security. All it took was his signature on a couple of forms. All he had to do was make one false accusation, and suddenly I was facing up to ninety days in the hole without any justification. To the hole I went.

•

I've dedicated my life, and this book, to inspiring people to ask more of themselves and more of the world. I have asked you to claim your past, hope as a child, embrace change, steel your determination, and believe in yourself. These are the steps along the path to becoming the person you want to be. I would be doing you a great disservice, however, if I did not take a few of chapters to warn you about the obstacles that you may still have ahead. Unfortunately, they often pop up when you least expect them.

By the time the new warden had come to FCI Florence, I thought I had been through the toughest part of the challenge. I had become a different person altogether. I was clean. I was a positive role model for my son and fellow inmates. I had regained my self-worth and dignity. I was doing something special.

I think that might be where I was going wrong in the warden's eye.

I'm sure that there was a fear of the special privileges. If I had special privileges, everyone would want them. Actually, that was already the case. I was commonly approached by inmates asking if I could help them do what I was doing. Sure, some of them were in it for the con (and I could spot them a million miles away), but others truly wanted to better themselves. They wanted to have the same opportunity I had. Of course, this begs the question, why not give it to them? I've already touched on the statistics of the educated ex-con. What if, at this point, the warden had taken advantage of my work to hold me up as a model to the other prisoners? What if he used me to encourage the other prisoners to better themselves? Might he have been considered a leader? A role model to wardens across the country for having the foresight to see that education could help rehabilitate criminals? We'll never know. He took the easy path and flexed his muscles rather than using his brain.

In Australia they have this saying. If the guy down the street starts acting above his station or gets too big for his britches, they'll say, "Ol' so and so is being a tall poppy." Basically what they mean is that if someone sticks their head up above the crowd, they are just begging to get cut down. I think that is what the warden thought of me. In his eyes, I was the same addict and bank robber that my file told him I was, and he wanted to remind me of it. Bank robbers don't get extra computer time or special privileges, they get hard time. Drug addicts don't get video courses and college degrees, they get all the punishment the system can dish out. And, prosecuted felons do not—I repeat, do *not*—question wardens about how they will run their prison, either directly or through a bunch of fancy suits on the outside. I was a tall poppy and he was going to mow me down.

People will try to sabotage you. Do not let them. It generally has nothing to do with what you are actually trying to accomplish with your own life, but rather, what it represents to the person who is trying to take your power away. For the warden it was a way to assert his authority in the prison. For others, sabotaging your successes can be a way to make them feel better about their own failures.

A friend once told me about an Oprah Winfrey show that she saw when Oprah first lost all of her weight. Here Oprah had finally accomplished this goal that she had set for herself, and what did she get in return? Bags of mail from people who said they weren't going to watch her show anymore. She had changed. She was no longer like them. These people did not hold her up as a role model, a winner of a tough battle. They lashed out in bitterness in an attempt to make their own failures her fault. She had risen above her place and they were going to try to make her feel like less of a person. It was because she had a personal chef. It was because she had a personal trainer. It was because she had money. She was not better than them. She should not get to be happy about her success. She hadn't earned it. She was just rich. They took it as a personal affront that she had succeeded where they were failing when, in reality, her weight loss had nothing to do with them. They just used it as justification to stay miserable in their own weight issues rather than do anything about them: "I could do it, too," they claimed, "if I could afford a personal chef and a personal trainer."

There may be those who will lash out at you for bettering yourself as well. They may try to sabotage your success, try to make you feel like a traitor, or attempt to take you down a peg. On the bright side, such criticism probably won't come in the quantities Oprah had to deal with. However, a single rejection can carry just as much weight, even more, if it comes from a friend or loved one.

From a friend or relative, someone you trust, someone who is supposed to treat you with love, being denounced as a "tall poppy" simply for reaching for a dream can be absolutely devastating. If, rather than lashing out directly, they use your relationship to try to sabotage you, it can be downright heartbreaking.

I have been in drug rehabilitation three times in my life. All three were before I went to prison and all three times I failed to be rehabilitated. At first I bought into the program and thought, *This is it. I'm really going to try to do it this time.* Each time, I would walk out of rehab clear-headed, a new man. And each time, all of my wonderful drug-addicted friends would throw me a great big congratulatory party filled with enough drugs to kill me dozens of times over. My friends. My "friends."

When I was younger, I was out with a group of my "friends" trespassing at a local reservoir because we were high on LSD and decided that we wanted to go swimming. My friend Paul was decked out in his usual cutoffs and favorite Aerosmith belt buckle, life of the party as usual. Just for the fun of it, he decided that he was going to climb an electrical tower. When he reached the top, he extended his arm out and deliberately touched the transformer. In an instant, a bolt of electricity shot through his arm and came out three gaping exit wounds that were instantly cauterized by the lightning. The electricity stopped his heart and he fell sixty feet to the ground. He lay there on the ground in front of us, eyes rolled up in his head, flopping like a fish.

Most of us ditched the scene. We called the paramedics and sent them over to see if they could help Paul, but none of us stuck around to go with him to the hospital.

One of the group, a guy named Jack, absolutely lost it and ran off into the woods. He stumbled around for four hours before finding his way to the police to tell them what had happened. By the time they investigated, Paul had been taken to the hospital and the scene had been cleaned up. For quite a few hours, Jack didn't know if he had actually seen his friend nearly fried to death or if he had hallucinated the whole thing.

In the end, Paul only survived because when he hit the ground after falling sixty feet, the impact restarted his heart.

At the time, that wasn't enough to stop a single one of us from using drugs. Instead, we tried to sneak some pot into to the hospital for him so that he could take a few hits while he recovered from his near-death experience.

In 2004, I did a speaking engagement in Colorado and tried to look up some of my old friends. Two were dead, three were in prison, others had been lost in the wind. Out of the entire group, only three of us had turned our lives around—the three who had ditched the group and the drugs.

My point is this: If your friends are not helping you to succeed, they are helping you to fail. They are not your friends.

So right about now, you may be saying, "Troy, what are you doing? I was so excited, I was so motivated, and you're telling me that the world is against me."

But if I didn't tell you these things, I'd be selling you a bill of goods. I've told you about the steps that you can take to become the person you want to be. Let's just consider this chapter a sturdy pair of walking boots to protect against sprained ankles.

Hopefully, you have surrounded yourself with people who want the best for you. If so, you've just gained some added strength in your fight. If not, here's a chance to do some weeding of your own. There are people who are going to see your head rising above the others in the poppy field and not like it. If they are your "friends," be prepared to leave them behind. They are not your friends.

If they are strangers who, for whatever reason, have decided to try to derail your dreams, don't let them; that is not their right.

Steel yourself, stick to your path, and march forward with determination. This is the point where some people will want to give up and lay down lest they be cut down. Me? I took one of my books with me to the hole.

Chapter 7

From Hole to Whole

What lies behind us, and what lies before us are tiny matters, compared to what lies within us.

—RALPH WALDO EMERSON

THE "HOLE" WAS a six-by-nine-foot cell containing a steel bunk bed, a stainless-steel toilet connected to a stainless-steel sink, and a stainless-steel shower. I was locked in this cell for twenty-four hours a day, with the exception of the one hour a day when I was sometimes—and I want to reiterate, sometimes—let out to pace back and forth in what looked like a small dog kennel. If I was lucky, I didn't have to share the space with a roommate.

There were several of these cells lined up in an isolated part of the prison. The people housed in the cells were the troublemakers of the institution; many of them were mentally challenged and probably shouldn't have been within the confines of a traditional prison setting. Hour after hour, day after day, week after week they would beat on the doors and scream. There was never a quiet moment. I never got any proper rest, but instead learned to catch a few winks whenever it subsided to a dull roar.

The steel door that provided the entrance into the cell contained a small slot in the center, through which the guards would slide food trays. As I stated previously, many of those sent to the hole were looking for trouble. You could be minding your own business and the next thing you know, your psychopath roommate decides it's a good idea to throw a cup full of urine and feces in the guards' faces when they open up the slot to give you your meal.

What do the guards do? They do what most of us would if that were done to us. They "suit up" and come in with their batons. You didn't have any control over who your cellmate was when you were in the hole, and you had to hope he didn't decide to pull this, because if he did you would take the beating right along with him. The guards didn't know whose arm it was that came out of that slot, and frankly they really didn't care. To make things worse, for the next two weeks, at least, that slot wasn't staying open for very long. Food trays were coming in on the fly. I don't know how you feel about eating food off a concrete floor shared by a human waste-tosser, but believe me, when you're hungry enough you'll eat food off anything.

As bad as this all was, it was not the worst of what I had to endure. The worst part was not knowing what my family, friends, scholarship committees, and teachers were being told. All I knew was that I was considered a "risk to the security of the institution" and that my case was under review.

I talked before about the value I place on my own integrity. I had worked very hard over the past six years to create hope and optimism against the proof of history, love, and trust instead of hurt and anger, a glimmer of a future in the place of a suicidal past. It was as fragile as a vase that had been smashed and glued back together. I did not think it could handle a blow like this.

I knew, and I can't blame them for this, that most of the people rooting for me had a little voice in the back of their heads telling them not to get too invested or too hopeful, because I could still let them down at any instant. The entire time I was in the hole, my mind was filled with conversations that I thought they must be having.

Without a doubt, everyone would believe the warden over me. After all, why wouldn't they just naturally accept that I had found trouble once again? I could see the anger on my dad's face and the tears in my mother's eyes as clearly as if they had been standing right in front of me. That's how I spent my time. Whenever I could not distract my mind with the book that I was reading multiple times over or busy myself with thinking about actual schoolwork, I tortured myself with countless conversations played out in my head about how Troy had let everyone down again.

Because I was in the hole, they didn't have to let any mail that I sent leave the prison and they didn't have to let any reach me. I could imagine my family's letters going unanswered and them assuming the worst. I knew for a fact that I had failed to complete the classes that I was taking and doubted I would be allowed to make them up. "Sorry, Professor, I couldn't finish my assignment because I got sent to the hole." Not exactly the conversation you want to have with your professor. Of course, that, along with my current situation, was sure to be reported to my scholarship committee. My funding would be gone for good.

The way I saw it, the vase I had rebuilt and protected for the past six years was smashing to the floor in front of my eyes.

For two months that was my torture. Sixty days of living in a tiny cage along with the animals of FCI Florence. I was losing weight, I had become pale, and I had read the same book six times. Up to that point I had always believed that things happened for a reason, but I have to tell you my faith was being tested. I had believed for the past six years that I could learn something from any situation I was placed in, but at that point, the little voice was starting to come through again: *Why is this happening to you, Troy? All you're trying to do is improve yourself, all you're trying to do is give yourself a chance to succeed when you're released, all you're trying to do is get an education. Why is this happening? Why do you even bother?*

I was told I was under investigation, but no one would tell me for what. I was faced with the possibility of at least another thirty days before anyone even had to review my situation. And then it happened. The only thing that could make the situation any worse. They informed me that I was being shipped to FCI Englewood, the oldest, nastiest prison within the Federal Bureau of Prisons. Built in 1939, it was like something out of a medieval movie. I was being shipped to the armpit of prisons.

As it turned out, what I thought was the worst news I could have received turned out to be my family and friends coming to the rescue. All of the conversations that I had made up in my head—my father's anger, my mother's tears—couldn't have been further from the truth.

In reality, my family and friends grew suspicious of my circumstances as soon as they heard that I had been sent to the hole. Not only did they not believe a word of it, but the more they received the runaround from the warden, the more concerned they grew.

My family and friends, including those well-connected friends on the scholarship committee, started calling up their friends, and their friends called their friends. Twenty-eight senators and congressmen, including Strom Thurmond and Newt Gingrich, along with the Head of the Federal Bureau of Prisoners, were apprised of my situation, and they all made calls to the warden. In the end, the situation started to gain such a high profile that the warden decided to eliminate the problem as quickly as he could by transferring me to another prison.

I was released from the hole to find that not only was my fragile vase still intact, but for the first time in twenty years, my friends and family had assumed the best of me rather than the worst.

Of course, it wasn't all smooth sailing from there. I was quickly shipped off to FCI Englewood. Shifted like cattle from one pen to another, I was informed that asbestos removal was making things tighter than usual. Within the individual housing units, 150 inmates shared a pod consisting of a common area and individual cubes. The common area was approximately twenty-by-forty feet and housed four showers, three sinks, three toilets, and a microwave oven. No stalls, no privacy, barely any room to breathe. On the east wall men were taking showers, on the north wall men were using the bathroom, on the west wall men were brushing their teeth, and on the south men were lined up to heat their food in the microwave oven.

Take a moment to picture that. No stalls, just one large open area, and all of these different activities taking place right next to one another. Just over five square feet per prisoner, minus the space taken up by the five-star amenities. You could feel the room breathe.

Of course there was some respite, if you could call it that. I was also assigned to a cube. Within this small cube (which I would estimate to be ten-by-twelve feet) there were three sets of bunk beds to accommodate my five lovely cellmates and me. My experience at FCI Florence had taught me that it was hard enough to find one guy you could let your guard down around. I couldn't even imagine what this was going to be like.

I was in this setting for only a short time before the realization set in that there was no way I could spend the next five years in those conditions. Again came the voice: *Why have you been singled out, Troy? Why have you been moved to such a horrible place? How are you going to serve the rest of this time?* I tried to keep my outlook as positive as possible. The only way I knew how to do that was to start over again. I needed to feel myself working toward my goals; otherwise, the reality of my new conditions, just better than those in the hole, would start to affect me. I concentrated on staying positive and on the tasks at hand to get me back on track. All the while I was trying to control the voice.

Of course, there was plenty to do because, in many ways, I had to start from scratch. First, I had to get permission from Englewood's educational coordinator. I had been in the middle of my last two courses when I was thrown in the hole, so I filled out the paperwork to get my books and coursework sent to me. I also had to write to the school to get permission to resume the classes and convince them to make a special exception for me so that I could complete the class without the videos I would have been required to watch. After about a month, I received the permissions that I needed, but was informed that all of my coursework and books had been "lost" in the transfer. Of course, I've always suspected they were probably "lost" the first day that I was thrown in the hole, but regardless of what happened to them, I was responsible for that work and I needed the books to do it. So I had to repurchase the books, which anyone who has ever had to purchase a textbook knows is not cheap, and I had to rewrite all of the papers I had completed during the first half of the course.

My work area was a desk in the corner similar to the one in the previous facility. At FCI Florence, however, I had only had one roommate to share a desk with, and we worked opposite shifts at the prison furniture plant. At FCI Englewood, I shared with five people who were constantly coming or going. Whether they were writing letters home or doing some other activity that required the use of the desk, I soon found that sometimes sitting on the floor with my books and papers piled around me had to be good enough.

It took me three months to finish my classes and get my second degree. The little voice was starting to get fainter, and I was beginning to contemplate my master's degree again, when I heard my name called over the intercom: "Evans #24291-013, report to the records office immediately." The lady at the records office told me to shut the door and sit down. I would later discover that FCI Englewood is the only institution within the Federal Bureau of Prisons that operates under the policy that saved me, the only institution in the entire nation that automatically reviews the sentence computation of every inmate that is transferred into their facility via another facility. She told me she had just gotten off the phone with the regional office, and in reviewing my sentence computation she had found that there was a mistake. I should not have been sentenced to thirteen years. I should have only been sentenced to eight. I was going home in ten days.

•

I just summarized that whole experience in a few brief paragraphs. Possibly the most important six months of my life, and it probably didn't take you more than ten minutes to read. The most crucial, desperate moment in my transformation, and we just blew right by it. But there was a warning there: You will be tested, and you will have to choose to pass.

That was the second time in my life that I had everything torn away from me. I remember the day that my father came home and told us we were moving like it was yesterday. I remember it because that was the first time in my young life that I learned that life is not fair.

Let's take a moment to get that thought out of the way, because many of us go through life absolutely paralyzed by it. Life is not fair and every moment spent in the contemplation of whether your circumstances are fair is another moment wasted. You can analyze your situation until you are blue in the face and complain to your best friend that it isn't fair or that it's unjust. But fact of the matter is, what has happened to you doesn't matter anymore. There is nothing that you can do about it. It is now a constant chapter in your history that will never change, and every moment that you spend contemplating it is another moment lost to dead time.

Do you remember the quote at the top of the preface of this book? *It is not important how we come to the events in our life. What is important is how we deal with those events.*

The day my father came home and told our entire family that we were moving to a strange new town, I had my foundation ripped out from under me. In my fourteen-year-old estimation, it was the same as if I had been sent to the hole or transferred to the worst kind of prison. I was going to a place I didn't want to go, for no good reason, to be around people that I didn't want to be around. I was being ripped from a place of security, encouragement, and success and being tossed into the unknown.

What did I do? I spent the next fifteen years of my life letting my future disintegrate while I rotted my brain with drugs, all the while absolving myself of any blame. Why? Because it wasn't fair. I absolutely wallowed in that thought and then compounded it with my drug paranoia. My grades weren't fair. Being denied play time and getting cut from the team weren't fair. The way my parents treated me wasn't fair.

Deep down, I knew I deserved at least some of what I was getting, but I could trace it all back to that move, and that made it easy to believe that I wasn't truly to blame for my circumstances. What my father had done to me was not fair, and throughout my teenage years my behavior was like a voice that was screaming at him the entire time:

"You had no right. I'll show you.

"You think you can take your fancy job and uproot our entire family?

"I'll show you.

"You're going to spend weeks on end out of town?

"I'll show you.

"You think that we'll all act like the Cleavers so that you can pretend to have the perfect life for your co-workers?

"I'll show you.

"You think you can control me, discipline me, make me be the son that you want?

"I'll show you."

I showed him right up until the point that I was facedown on the ground in shorts and flip-flops, being arrested for armed robbery.

How I wish I could go back and talk to my fourteen-year-old self.

I will tell you now what I would tell that young man: The things that happen in life don't change the "core you" unless you let them.

I don't think that I deliberately set off down a path to self-destruction, but once I had gotten myself into a little bit of trouble, I let my circumstances be excuses to continue down the wrong path. I saw the look on my old man's face and I thought, *This hurts you, huh? Good.* I spent so much time feeling sorry for myself that I never even realized that it wasn't my dad or the move that ruined me. It was me.

In the first part of this book, I talked about finding your hope and building momentum, but when I was sent to the hole and then transferred to FCI Englewood, my hopes were challenged, my momentum was taken, and my path was blocked. For the first time in years, I was hearing that little voice again, questioning my path and my ability to continue my journey. My power, my hopes, and my future were being taken from me. I was facing another five years in one of the worst prisons in the U.S., and for the first time in years I started to notice who was dealing drugs inside and how I could get them.

Those situations, the really tough ones that seem to take away all hope and often come up on you in the blink of an eye, are tests, and tests are meant to be hard. I had to choose to pass that test. I had to look desperate times in the face and say, "I am not the person I once was and no matter how difficult life becomes, I will no longer choose that easy path, because nothing in life that is worthwhile is ever easy." If I had let my power be taken, if I had gone back to serving dead time, if I had turned back to drugs, the Troy Evans released from FCI Englewood three months later would have been a different person altogether. In those three months, I could have thrown it all away.

On the other hand, if I had only chosen the better path when I was a kid, I could have been a pro ball player. I'd be able to travel to Australia and New Zealand (ex-cons are not allowed in those countries). I could take my son hunting (I'm not allowed to own a firearm). I would have had my entire life to fill with all of the successes I could muster rather than losing twenty-two and a half years to drugs and prison time.

You, too, will be tested. There will be times when you will lose your path. There will be times when you make a choice and find yourself on the wrong path, and there will be times when you lose your path due to circumstances beyond your control. When this happens, you will be tempted to lose hope. You may find yourself slipping into a spiral of self-loathing or cynicism.

I cannot give you a map to move forward when you lose your path, but a map does exist. It is the one you will draw as you travel. It may not be able to tell you how to move forward, but it can tell you where you've been. My advice is, if and when you do lose your way, there is never any shame in starting over. In fact, that is often the best way to get back on your path. Go back to the point that you last knew you were on the right track and start again. I had to start the permission process all over again at FCI Englewood. I even had to redo several of my assignments. But while I was retracing my steps to get back on the right path, I was choosing to pass my test. The same will be true for you. There is no such thing as absolute failure unless you choose it by giving up. Choose to succeed.

Chapter 8

Passing Through Open Gates

Any fact facing us is not as important as our attitude toward it, for that determines our success or failure.

—DR. NORMAN VINCENT PEALE

THE MOMENT OF MY RELEASE, I was filled with overwhelming happiness. I had learned valuable lessons and I had succeeded. I was drug-free and educated, I had my family back, and I had my whole life ahead of me. But I soon found out that freedom itself was a challenge.

The first night of my release, my sister picked me up at the gates a free man for the first time in many, many years. It was an extremely strange feeling to come and go as I wanted. There were trees around me, a dog ran by, I heard a kid laugh, and I had an ice cream cone. To celebrate, my sister took me to downtown Denver for dinner and introduced me to sushi. I had never heard of such a thing and the thought seemed repugnant, but compared to what I had been fed for the last several years I knew there was no way it could kill me. She dropped me off in the middle of downtown Denver as she went to park the car. There I stood, lights flashing, cars passing, crowds of people walking by me. The stimulation was overwhelming. I couldn't move. It was like I was frozen in time, like I wasn't even there. As my sister approached she said I had the strangest look on my face, a look of fascination and fear.

The comings and goings of the free world were something I hadn't witnessed for years. I knew guys who returned to prison of their own free will after purposely violating their parole because they could not take the real world. They were institutionalized. Having been told what to do and when to do it for so many years, they couldn't make decisions for themselves. We heard stories of trips to the grocery store that would leave a grown man completely overwhelmed by the choices in, for example, cereal, only to realize that he had been standing in the aisle for an hour without making a decision. It is an amazing feeling to fear a thing like Cocoa Puffs. Was this going to happen to me? I had no idea what to expect.

Generally when prisoners are released, they're assigned to a halfway house, a place that is meant to help you get your feet on the ground as you re-assimilate into the world. Halfway houses have several rules designed to help keep you out of trouble. Even more importantly, they help your parole officer keep an eye on you when you are released.

Because of my strangely sudden release, the state did not have any room available for me in a halfway house, as would normally have been the case. Instead, my parents went through a fairly intense process of evaluation to allow me to return to their home.

For the first few months, I kept to myself for the most part and continued the life that I knew. I would run in the morning, lift weights in the afternoon, and run again in the evening. I filled the hours in between sitting at my desk writing my résumé or monitoring the stock market. The whole time, I wandered the house, unnerving my parents with the way I would just meander from room to room without a purpose, as if I were still pacing a cell. Years later, they commented that my face had looked haunted. They didn't quite know what to do with me, and that made three of us.

To further complicate the situation, I was still being watched. I was well aware upon my release that I would be on probation and subjected to surprise inspections, drug tests, and ongoing scrutiny by a parole officer. Compared to another five years in prison, that seemed like a blessing. The eyes that kept me continually off balance were actually much closer than that. I was in my parents' home. The last time I had been under their roof, I was high, lying, stealing, disrupting the family, and breaking every promise I'd ever made to them. When I was locked up, it was easier for them to trust me. But out in the real world, where I was faced with real-world temptations, no matter how hard they tried they just couldn't fully trust me.

I made my decision right then to embrace once again the changes that had been laid before me. I made a list of things I wanted to accomplish and immediately set about trying to complete the entire thing. I was no longer stagnant, I was hyper-committed. There was no such thing as down time to me. No such thing as time off. Every moment that I was awake, from early morning to late at night, was spent working toward something on my list. I felt a compulsion to constantly prove that I wasn't an imposter; I truly did belong in the outside world. I thought I was being watched all of the time, so it was absolutely paramount to me that I be seen showing focus and commitment at all times.

See how hard I'm working! See how many hours I spend committed to my goals! See that I am keeping my nose clean!

One day I woke up from my daily ritual and realized I had become the model prisoner all over again. Here I was with access to the outside world. I could walk barefoot through the grass, see a movie, go to the park. . . . I could do anything I wanted, yet I hadn't really allowed myself a single freedom.

I had to get out in the world. I had to leave Evans #24291-013 behind and start figuring out who Troy Evans was.

I found employment through a local temp agency, and at the same time began working for a member of the National Speakers Association. The temp agency work was a means of making money, but through the work with the speaker, I was building a foundation for giving a previously discarded life new value. While in prison, I had begun to build my worth again through my relationship with my family, and yet there was a world of potential I had thrown away when I was fourteen that I needed to make up for. I had taken the wrong path. I couldn't turn back time, but I could give that lost time meaning. I thought that if I could use my experiences to spare even one person the pain that I put myself and my family through, then I could give purpose to all of the years I had lost. Call it Fate, Karma, or Divine Intervention, but I felt that there was a reason that the National Speakers Association had been the group to take a chance on me all those years before. I needed a path and this one seemed clear to me.

I worked in a furniture factory from 4 A.M. until 12 P.M. (doing their accounting, of all things), and then I would head over to my mentor's to put in another full day's work, helping him with scheduling, answering phone calls, and whatever else he needed before working with him to write the first drafts of speeches I still give today. Between the two, I was finally starting to live again. I had a purpose that wasn't based on the sheer mechanics of living life, and in the meantime, I had started to do the things that normal people did, like managing to save enough money to buy my first car. It probably wasn't much to look at from an outsider's perspective, a ten-year-old Acura Legend, but it was my first step toward true freedom.

I had created some momentum in the outside world, but what I truly craved was my own space. Nothing fantastic. All I needed was a space of my own that gave me some privacy; a place where I could go to sleep at night and feel safe; a place where I could have some time with my new girlfriend. In short, some place that was not my parents' house.

The day I walked into my own apartment for the first time was the day I truly had my first taste of freedom. From there, everything started to click for me.

I started to feel more comfortable around strangers. I could go to the mall and not panic when I saw a group of people walking toward me. I started to change my own personal culture from that of a con, who had to constantly be on guard for the next life-threatening event, to a free man. That may seem strange, but for many months, the things I craved most on the outside—human interaction, normal conversation, a safe environment—were beyond my grasp because I couldn't shake the thousand-mile stare. Looking back, I'm certain that what I had was some sort of post-traumatic stress. I couldn't put everyday things in the right frame of reference. Groups of people were gangs, it didn't matter if they were all eighty years old and had walkers. I was suspicious of them because they were in groups. People walking behind me in the mall might have shanks. I generally turned around to find a teenager with a pink cell phone or something equally ridiculous, but I couldn't shake my uneasiness.

When I moved into my own place, that final shift took place. Now I wanted to be around other people. My girlfriend used to tease me that I couldn't cross the room without stopping to have some involved conversation with a perfect stranger. I had been without that sort of normal interaction for so long, I couldn't get enough of it.

It wasn't just the people, either. It was everything. Every day, whether I was doing something new or something completely routine, I would find myself stopping to wonder why I had never realized how special the world was, how beautiful flowers were, how gratifying it was to watch children play, how soothing it was to lie in the shade. I was thirty-five years old and it was like I had never done these things before in my life.

Then I started my journey to the pinnacle of my freedom. My mentor took me aside and told me that I was ready to go out on my own and begin my career as a professional speaker. It was barely more than a year since my release, and suddenly I was on planes to different parts of the country, I was meeting more people in one day than I would have thought possible, I was touching the lives of more people in one day than I ever could have hoped to. I was being paid to tell my story. I had complimentary meals and hotels and standing ovations. And this is the big one: I was being paid compliments by people left and right. I was laying my entire past out for the public to scrutinize as they would and I was being thanked for having made a difference. This was the true purpose of my journey. I had turned my life around; I had gone from desperation to dedication, and I was becoming the man I wanted to be.

It wasn't an easy trip; I had to embrace change at almost every turn. But this time I had my friends and family there to give me support.

Freedom was an awesome thing and it was meant to be a little scary to me. I had to relearn freedom from the standpoint of a sober, law-abiding citizen. I had to have it revealed to me in shocking clarity so that I would know that every moment I spent as a free man had amazing things in store for me. Becoming educated and surviving prison were only short parts of my path. Once I got out, I found that there would always be another challenge, another obstacle to overcome, another lesson to learn. I found that I was better than I had been, but I was still not the best I could be. This will always be true.

That is the warning in this chapter. You must learn to love the path you take toward your goals, because at the end of each path is the beginning of a new one. In the preface of this book, I told you about Janus, the god of gates and the god of beginnings, who is depicted with two faces so that he can look forward and backward. When you have reached one goal, you will have a choice to make between continuing on a new path and slipping back into dead time. In life, I will meet Janus again and again, because as soon as I accomplish one goal, another must replace it. Each time I meet him another test is passed and another lesson is learned. Dead time is no longer good enough for me, nor, I hope, will it be good enough for you.

•

Not all of the gates I pass are huge and imposing, and yours won't be either, but sometimes the smallest challenges can still hold great lessons.

Upon my release, I discovered I could not get auto insurance because

I didn't have an insurance record for three years prior. Where I live, under state law, if you can't show proof of insurance for the prior three years it is illegal for the insurance companies to issue you a policy. This was intended to catch people who'd been driving without insurance, but left no loophole for someone such as myself, who hadn't needed to carry insurance. Phone calls, letter writing, and appealing my situation seemed to make no difference to anyone I contacted, and I was finally forced into informing an insurance company that the place I resided for the past three years did not require drivers to carry insurance. From that, I learned that there actually are still people in the world who prefer to think the best of you rather than the worst. I never said where I had been, but they were happy to assume I had been in a foreign country. I'm sure that prison never crossed their minds. After years in the detention system, it was nice to finally be given the benefit of the doubt rather than the nightstick of unfounded assumption.

Upon obtaining insurance I tried to secure a driver's license, but was told I had to resolve a ten-year-old violation in another state before my residing state would issue a license. Hence another six weeks of red tape and paperwork passed before I was finally issued my driver's license. It forced me to remember that no matter who I became, I would always have to be accountable for my past.

I then attempted to rebuild my credit, but the bankers were shocked to see that not only did I lack a recent credit history, but my credit report was actually completely blank, as if I had dropped off the face of the Earth. I was informed that this was more damaging than having a bad credit report. I would have been better off showing a bankruptcy, a repossessed vehicle, anything. From that I learned that even a clean slate could present a challenge.

Of course, your credit report is the only place where you're better off having a marred past. Inform someone that you spent the last several years incarcerated for armed bank robbery, and the reception is usually very cool. I learned quickly that it was better if people got to know me first, before I shared the details of my recent residence with them. Only then were they willing to look beyond the stigma to who I really was.

Easy times after my release? No. Worth working for and fighting through? Yes. That which is worthwhile in our life, which is really worthwhile, is never going to be easy. My dead time is over, and every day, I choose a better life.

Chapter 9

Letting Go of the Life Sentence

We did what we knew. When we knew better, we did better.

—MAYA ANGELOU

I MENTIONED BEFORE THAT WHEN I was released, it was under special circumstances. It was uncommon that I was to go live with my parents. Since the halfway house option was not available, my parole officer was sent over to my parents' house to assess the environment. He interrogated them, opened drawers, searched for firearms, and treated them with a sense of overall disdain. After all, their son was a drug-addicted bank robber.

That was when my dad truly realized what it meant for me to be coming to his house. Up to that point, it had meant only excitement and celebration. I had been released five years early. His son, who had turned his life around, earned two degrees, and kicked drugs for good, was coming home. But, when he and my mother were put under the scrutiny of an officer of the court, it all came rushing back to him—the nights they spent worrying about me the last time I lived under their roof, the lying, the stealing, the heartache, the pain. He had let that happen under his roof once already and he'd be damned if he was going to let it happen again.

I had just had a conversation with my dad about how exciting my latest turn of events was, and the next thing I knew, I was on the phone with him again, but this time he was lambasting me like I was still back in high school. He started laying down ground rules about curfews, respecting his house, staying away from drugs, getting a job, becoming a productive member of society. He had been fooled by me before and he wanted me to know that he wasn't going to take any funny business this time.

Well, I hung up the phone and thought about it for a minute, and for the first time since the news of my early release, I realized that being freed from prison did not mean that my sentence was over. Then I thought about it for a few more minutes and decided that I was not going to allow myself to be pigeonholed by my past for the rest of my life. I called him right back and told him that I was not a kid anymore. I was not going to be talked to like that. I felt that I had proved that I was a changed man, and I was not going to sit idly by and let him treat me as if there were no difference between the Troy Evans who entered prison and the Troy Evans who would be leaving it. If he had a problem with it, I'd find someplace else to go.

We got off the phone, and a few days later, I received a letter from him. In it, he explained to me what I had done to him, my mother, and my brother and sister. He told me about all of the years of hurt I had caused them, all of the tears they had cried, the number of times they had blamed themselves, and the sorrow with which they had to let go of me when they knew I was on a path of destruction.

I read that letter over and over again, and I realized that it was not up to me to determine when my sentence would be over. I had harmed many people in my life, and until they chose to forgive me, I would not be released. All I could do was wake up each day, committed to showing them through my actions that I was a changed man who might, someday, be worthy of their forgiveness, without letting their feelings define who I was in the meantime.

As if to punctuate that point, I was soon released and went to meet my first parole officer. My parents had warned me, but I was not prepared for that first encounter. He promptly informed me that he was looking to send me right back to prison. He said that he knew my kind and if I so much as stepped one toe outside the line, he had absolutely no compunction about taking me back in so fast my head would spin.

I told him that the most valuable thing to me in the world was my liberty and that he would have absolutely nothing to worry about from me. Over the next year, I set out to prove that statement to be nothing short of the absolute truth.

During that year, my dad learned that he didn't have anything to worry about either. I was the model prisoner/houseguest, if a little too intense about everything that I needed to accomplish. Our dinner table once again buzzed with the day's recap, but it was still a bit strained. I found myself wondering if I would ever have a really good relationship with my father again.

In an effort to show him and my mother progress, I invited them both to one of the first speaking engagements that I landed in Phoenix. He and my mother sat in the audience and heard me tell my story. I led a room full of perfect strangers through my transformation from the perfect son into the monster who hurt everyone that he loved. I publicly acknowledged that I was the one responsible for the choices that I made in my life, and I shared the pain that I would have to live with for the rest of my life, knowing what I had done to both those I loved and strangers alike.

At the end of the presentation, when I went to ask my mom and dad what they thought, I found them with tears in their eyes. My dad gave me a hug and I knew instantly that as far as he was concerned, my sentence was over. He just needed to know that I understood his pain. Once he saw that he didn't have to keep showing it to me, he was able to let it go. He was released from his own life sentence of pain and guilt and given back the son he loved so much.

That was the first day of a fantastic friendship that has blossomed between my dad and me. It was the first day that I knew that I was completely forgiven and the first day I knew that I had my dad back.

So I won over my dad, who was essentially my warden in those days, since I was living under his roof. I still had some work to do with my parole officer, but things had been getting better and better there as well. My PO soon found out that I was a cakewalk assignment. I was always where I told him that I would be, I never popped positive on my drug tests, and I was constantly employed. In fact, the only way I ever inconvenienced him was by becoming too successful. It didn't take long before I was getting speaking engagements all over the country. As a condition of my parole, I could travel, but before I left the state I had to have permission forms signed by my PO.

There were times when my PO was out sick or on vacation and my forms sat on his desk while I frantically called his office. I needed to be on a plane and I didn't have permission. My career and parole both rested on the chance that I would be able to find someone to roust him out of bed or sign the forms for him so that I could make my flight. It was frenzied at times, but we had reached an understanding that allowed me to pursue my dream of speaking.

I was just starting to settle into the routine when it was all turned upside down again. The office was restructuring and I was being reassigned.

I couldn't envision a worse problem. I had spent an entire year cracking this tough nut to the point where we had an extremely easy relationship. He knew he could count on me, and in return, I never had to worry about being turned down for one of my trips. I begged and pleaded for him to find a way to make an exception so he could remain my PO, but his hands were tied, and I was given someone new.

This was a wake-up call to me. I was released in December of 1999 and given five years of supervised release. At this point, only one year had gone by, and already my case was being reassigned. I started to envision what it would be like if I had to win a new PO over every year in order to continue my work as a speaker. I shuddered to think that all it would take was one hard case to come in and, like the warden at FCI Florence, he or she could yank the entire rug out from under my feet. There was nothing I could do but hope. I already knew that life wasn't always fair. I decided that the only thing I could control was myself, so I resolved that I would just keep winning my new POs over until my five-year supervisory sentence was up.

My new PO was assigned to me just about the same time that I moved into my first apartment. She was a nice lady, but she read me the riot act during our first meeting just as my first PO had. For the next few months, I continued my role as Troy Evans, superstar parolee, in order to win her over. On the bright side, she caught on to me almost immediately. It wasn't long after she took over my case that she told me that, if I needed to travel and for some reason couldn't get a hold of her, to just go. She trusted me and we would work it out when I returned.

This was new. My first PO and I had a good relationship, but here I had an officer of the court, who was basically trained not to believe a word I said, actually going out of her way to be helpful. In fact, she was so confident in me once she got to know me that a full year went by without us meeting once.

Then, in December 2001, she called me out of the blue. "Troy," she said, "I need you to come in to the office."

"What for?" I asked.

"I'd rather tell you in person," she replied.

My face went white.

Let me give you a bit of history to explain my reaction. The only other time that I had been called into the PO office, I was sitting, waiting for my appointment on the bench outside of the office with another ex-con. We were chatting away about how we had been called in, when suddenly, two U.S. Marshalls came through the door, stood my benchmate up, and told him that his parole had been violated and he was going back to prison, while slapping on the cuffs. The guy never knew what hit him. Combine that with my original arrest experience in the hotel, and I was scared to death. I didn't know what I had done, but I was convinced that it was all over. The rug was being yanked, it had all been too good to be true, and I was going back to prison.

I said, "You're scaring me. Tell me what you want." And she continued with, "I'd rather tell you in person—just come in."

I swallowed hard and said, "I'm not coming. You tell me right now what is happening. Just tell me."

I could hear a sigh of resignation on the other end of the phone, and she said, "I wanted to give you your Christmas present. I've petitioned the court on your behalf. I talked to the judge and said that I have never seen nor heard of an ex-convict that has done as well as you have. I told him that it is a waste of the government's money to continue to supervise your parole and we should release you from the remainder of your parole obligation."

My jaw was on the ground. Apparently, the judge had had a similar reaction. In fact, it was the first time in his thirty-plus years on the bench that a parole officer had ever petitioned the court on behalf of one of her charges. That alone had him so convinced that I was worthy of special treatment that he granted her motion and gave me my best Christmas present ever. Yet another sentence had been lifted.

•

I wanted to take some time to share these stories with you because there is one more thing that I need to warn you about. Just because you change and know that you are a new you, do not expect that you will win everyone over immediately.

If you're changing something about yourself that hasn't affected anyone else in the past, then this warning may not be such a big deal to you. If, however, you are recovering from an addiction, changing the way you conduct your personal relationships, trying to improve yourself in your work environment, etc., it is going to take some time for people to get to know the new you.

There are few things as frustrating as a sentence you carry for things that you've done in the past, but in all fairness, you earned it. The people in your life will release you from it in their own time, and there is nothing you can do about that. The shame would be to let it affect you in your journey or taint the definition of who you are becoming. Some would say, "If that's what they think of me, then fine, that's who I'll be." Do not throw all your efforts away in a tantrum over something that you cannot possibly control. Stay the course, and know that if you continue to show them the new you through your actions, they will eventually come around.

Of course, they may not be the only ones that you have to worry about. I still struggle to this day with releasing myself from a self-inflicted life sentence. I stuck a gun in the faces of people who were only doing their jobs. For all I know, those tellers are still suffering from my actions today. I think about them having nightmares, post-traumatic stress, trouble working, and it plagues my conscience.

I would love to apologize to them, but it is against the law for me to contact any of my victims.

If you've wronged people in the past, as I have, you will never forget it, and frankly, some things shouldn't be forgotten. You have to own those actions. At the same time, it is important to learn how to live with your past without allowing it to define your future. You will never be able to give yourself the gift of reaching your full potential if you believe yourself to be unworthy of it.

I spent many sleepless nights thinking of those people and hating myself for what I had done. Finally, I wrote each of them a letter, explaining to them how I understood the damage I had caused and including my most sincere hope that I had not hurt them for a lifetime. I apologized from the bottom of my heart.

Since I couldn't send the letters to my victims, I folded them up into an envelope and mailed them to Santa Claus at the North Pole. Some day, I hope to gain a presidential pardon. If and when I do, my first order of business will be to send copies of those letters to the true recipients.

I will never forget what I've done, but I am not that person anymore. I had to find a way to be able to hate the man that I was without taking it out on the man that I've become. My life sentence may always be in the back of my mind, but I will not let it define who I am.

PART THREE

On Your Side

Though we travel the world over to find the beautiful, we must carry it with us or we find it not.

—Ralph Waldo Emerson

Chapter 10

Lock Up Your Loved Ones

All you need is love.

—JOHN LENNON

WHEN I DISCOVERED I was being released from prison five years earlier than I had expected, my family and I kept it a secret from my son, Eric. My release date was thirteen days before Christmas, so my parents quickly made arrangements for Eric to spend Christmas vacation with them in Phoenix. This didn't raise any red flags for Eric because he had been doing this every other year for the past seven years. On the day that my son flew into Phoenix Sky Harbor International Airport, my father, mother, brother, sister, and I drove down to greet Eric. My mother, father, and sister went to the gate where Eric was scheduled to arrive, and my brother and I stayed back four gates, I on one side of the hallway with a hat and sunglasses on, my brother on the other side with a video camera, taping the entire scene. As Eric got off the plane my parents and sister greeted him with hugs and kisses, and after exchanging pleasantries began heading in my direction. At this time, I stepped away from the wall and began walking toward them. As I approached them I stepped in front of the group and said, "Excuse me, could someone please tell me what time it is?" Out of the corner of my eye I could see my son's face, his mouth wide open and his eyes as big as saucers. Answering my question, my mom said, "It's 7:30." "Thank you very much," I said and stepped around them, continuing on. Behind me I could hear my son saying, "That was my dad!"

My father said, "That wasn't your dad, Eric, you know where your dad is." A second passed and my son said, "I'm telling you, Grandpa, that was my dad. Go get him!" That, of course, was all I could take, and I spun around, ran back to my son, and spent the next five minutes hugging, kissing, and crying. I definitely blew my boy right out of the water, and that was the first time in his entire life he had ever been rendered speechless.

•

Family and loved ones—there is absolutely nothing more important. This bears repeating. There is absolutely nothing more important in our lives than the people we love and those who love us. I am in particular talking about the people we see every day, the people we often take for granted: the ones who we assume will always be there, the ones who we peck on the cheek as we walk in the door after a long day, only then to plop our butts on the couch. The people who get that same gesture as we leave the next morning. The people who we assume are always going to be a part of our life, no matter what.

I'm here to tell you, they are not always going to be a part of our lives and they are not always going to be there. I didn't realize how important these people were until they were taken away from me.

Since my first foray into the world of drugs, I had let many of my loved ones escape from my life. Some of them I pushed away through anger, and some left because being too close to me was breaking their hearts. For every one of these special people, I had an excuse for why I didn't need them. My father was always riding me, my mom was being overdramatic, my brother and I were always fighting anyway, my ex-wife was a nag. These were the things that I told myself as I slowly chipped away at every close relationship I had.

When I sobered up and had prison bars placed between me and my loved ones, that's when I realized what I had done. Suddenly, I was facing a thirteen-year sentence, and I didn't know if there was a single person on the outside who wasn't happier to have me locked away. All of the reasons that I had for fighting with them instantly became insignificant, and I realized that I had been letting those relationships go when I should have been locking them up in my heart as tightly as I could.

If you want to know the value of your loved ones, imagine for just a moment what it would be like to lose them.

In prison, I was surrounded by more than a thousand inmates and guards, and I was, at all times, utterly alone. When you're in a situation that volatile, the fewer signs of weakness you show, the better off you are. You do not share your thoughts and feelings. You have no one to comfort you. You have truly lost your soft place to fall.

The only connection to that part of the life you used to know is mail call or the infrequent visitations that you might receive.

Mail call was a sight to see in prison. You could always tell it was getting close to mail call by the movement in the prison. It was almost like a tide being pulled by the moon—a subtle yet powerful force that, every day but Sunday, drew everyone to the area where the mail was distributed.

If you paid close attention, you could even catch the glimmer of an emotion coming from some of the inmates—a hint of hope, sometimes even a fragment of a smile on the face of an inmate whose name was called.

The truly sad thing was that, more often than not, the letters didn't even contain good news. We were the forgotten family members. Not many of the inmates had people who would bother with a letter unless there was something remarkable that needed to be relayed, such as a death in the family or a "Dear John" sentiment.

Even if you were, like me, one of the lucky ones who had some family willing to offer you support and correspondence, time passes in a different way on the outside. If I wrote a letter to a friend or family member, receiving it was one of the many things that had happened to them on that particular day. And let's face it, written correspondence has gone by the wayside since our grandparents' days. One of my letters might sit on my parents' kitchen table or desk for a week or more until they had a chance to sit down and write me back. That's how time works in the real world.

That is not the case in prison. In prison we've got nothing but time, and letters are the inmates' one link to the outside world. To me, and to the other inmates, that week or two or three might as well have been years. A few lines of mundane news about someone's life was like spun gold. It was a glimpse at the normal, the ability to share with someone like real humans do. It was contact with a loved one.

That is something that I can never take for granted again.

When we played that trick on my son, we were just trying to have a little good-natured fun, but what he gave me was yet another lesson in life—be vigilant in your love. My son had played second fiddle to drugs in his father's eyes for years, he had been through high-security prison searches, he had had to fend off countless attacks of ridicule for his father, but when we played the trick on him in the airport, he was still willing to argue with those he trusted—his own grandparents—to be vigilant in his love for his father. Because I had been in an emotional void for all of those years, that was the best gift he could have given me.

There was a guy I knew in prison who I'll call "Chuck." Chuck was a good guy as far as cons go—he minded his own business, was very respectful of others, never got in anybody's way, played centerfielder on my softball team. Chuck and I worked in UNICOR, Federal Prison Industries, a manufacturing facility within the institution. We built furniture. I worked upstairs in the business office; Chuck worked downstairs on the production floor assembling furniture. One day I walked over to the copier, and as my copy was running, I looked out the big plate glass window in front of me. On the concrete floor below lay my friend Chuck, a six-foot pool of blood surrounding his head. Standing over Chuck was another inmate with a four-foot oak table leg that he had used to bash in Chuck's head. Judging by the pool of blood, by the time I saw him, Chuck had been dead for some time. Thirty to forty other inmates stood in a circle around his limp body, having witnessed the whole thing. Nobody had lifted a hand to stop what they were seeing. Nobody called a guard. Everyone just walked away knowing that they could be in Chuck's place the next day, the next hour, the next minute.

Chuck lost his life that day because of a sixty-nine-cent writing pen. The assailant accused Chuck of walking by his workstation and picking up his pen, thus disrespecting him and giving him the right to take Chuck's life. Chuck had a wife of ten years, an eight-year-old daughter, and six weeks left on a six-year prison sentence. In that instant it was all snatched away. A father was lost, a widow was made, and a future vanished into thin air, all over a sixty-nine-cent pen.

I've often wondered what unfinished business Chuck had. After all, there were only six short weeks left before the world would be open to him again. Was he waiting for the right moment to tell his wife and daughter how much they really meant to him? Did he look forward to the day, six weeks down the road, when he would be able to start rebuilding those relationships? Was he waiting for the best time, place, and circumstances? If he were, he may have missed his opportunity altogether.

My point is this: Don't wait for something to happen to mend those bridges, rebuild your relationships, and bring your loved ones closer. Allowing yourself to lose a loved one to an argument, distance, or any other triviality is just plain criminal. If tomorrow were the last day of your life, would you have made your best effort in all of your relationships?

I have two younger siblings. My brother is two years younger than I, and my sister is four years younger. My sister and I have always had a great relationship. She was generally willing to see the best in me despite the life choices I was making. We remained close throughout my addiction, she was one of my staunchest supporters while I was in prison, and she was the one to pick me up when I was released.

My brother and I, on the other hand, had a tenuous relationship at best throughout most of our lives. When we were young, I think that he was often overshadowed by my successes. The things that came so easily to me—my grades, my athleticism—were things that he had to work much harder at. He would try his best, with absolute conviction, but he didn't have the natural gifts that brought successes so easily within my reach.

Once we moved and I began my downward spiral, the tides should have shifted in his favor. But while he stayed the course, I became such a disruption that rather than doting on his successes, as they had mine, my parents dubbed him the "son we don't have to worry about" and I continued to require all of their attention. I've already mentioned that I was a severe disruption in my parents' house. Every time I came home stoned, or fought with my parents, or occupied their time as they worried about what to do with me, I was stealing that time from my brother and sister. My brother was going through the same transition that I was when we moved, but he kept his nose clean, stayed in school, stayed off drugs, and graduated without ever causing a problem. I'm sure that he didn't want to add to my parents' torment. Of course, we all know the saying, "The squeaky wheel gets the grease." Well, I was squeaking at about a million decibels. I'm sure there were days that, no matter what my brother had accomplished, he didn't even make the household radar. It was all about Troy.

My brother went on to join the Navy and become an electrician. He never really made a point of hiding his contempt for me, and when I was younger and on drugs, living a fast life, I didn't care. My take on it was, "He hates me anyway, so screw him. I don't need a brother, especially a younger brother who gives me the same disapproving looks as my parents." That was how things were when I was sent to prison at the age of twenty-eight. We had spent the majority of our lives in the same house, we were of the same flesh and blood, but we barely spoke.

Years went by and I'm sure I confirmed every sentiment he had ever had about me when I went to prison. But then I started to turn my life around. He heard about my progress through the family grapevine, and one day, to my great astonishment, I was told that my brother had come to visit me. Our conversation was kept fairly cordial and mostly informational. He seemed to think it was strange that I was so shocked he would come see me. I told him I was glad he did. In truth, we didn't really know how to have that conversation. From the outside, I'm sure it seemed quite normal, if strained. But let me tell you what was happening on the inside.

I was years into my sentence at this point. I was living in a place where you didn't show weakness, you didn't show emotions, and you definitely didn't show tears. I was looking across the table at my brother, careful as always to keep from showing too much on my face, but inside my heart was exploding. Every new supporter I won over was a triumph, but this was my brother. The brother who I thought I had lost, who very justifiably had written me off years before, was here, talking to me about my schooling and how I was doing. I didn't just get a supporter that day; I learned that despite it all, my brother still loved me, had probably never stopped. I wanted to laugh and cry and hug him all at the same time. All I was allowed was to sit there and talk, and even though that had to be good enough, I knew that one day, we would have better moments together. I was going to keep on this path, because, in addition to all of the other goals I had, I knew then that I was going to win my brother back.

Years have passed and I have indeed won my brother back. In fact, we are best friends. We talk daily about our lives and sometimes I even get to give him some big-brotherly advice. I cherish that relationship every day and sometimes think about all of the things that could have gone wrong. I think about Chuck and cringe at the "what ifs" that could have prevented me from ever truly knowing how wonderful it is to have my brother in my life. No argument or sense of pride is worth that.

It is not *what* we have in our lives but *who* that matters, and we all need to ask ourselves if we are spending the *least* time with the people who are the *most* important. Let these people know you love them and let them know often. Make them feel special every day. Don't wait one more day lest it become too late. Regrets down the road are mistakes made today. Please don't ever take these people for granted.

I am fortunate enough to be surrounded by a family of people who, through trials and tribulations, have been vigilant in their love. When I was on drugs, they tried to intervene. When I lost touch, they didn't lose hope. When I was branded society's outcast, they hugged me tightest. When they were taken away from me, I finally knew their worth.

Let these people know you love them and let them know often. Let them know how special they are every day. Watch your kids and fight to protect them no matter how much they rebel against it. Pick up the phone and call your parents, or better yet, visit them; they will not always be there for you. Hug your loved ones close and be true to your commitments, and you will have that love reflected back to you. Lock up your loved ones so that you will never have to regret things not said or love not given. They will be your cheerleaders, your confidants, and your reality check. As you are there for them, they will be there for you. It will make a difference to them and it will make a difference in you.

Chapter 11

Do Time, Don't Let It Do You

We all have the same amount of time. You have the same amount of time as the average billionaire. It's not how much time you have, it's how you use the time you have.

—LARRY WINGET

- To realize the value of one year, ask the student who has failed his or her final exam.
- To realize the value of one month, ask the mother who has given birth to a premature baby.
- To realize the value of one week, ask the editor of a weekly newspaper.
- To realize the value of one day, ask the daily wage laborer with ten kids to feed.
- To realize the value of one hour, ask the lovers who are waiting to meet.
- To realize the value of one minute, ask the person who has missed the plane.
- To realize the value of one second, ask the person who has survived an accident.
- To realize the value of a millisecond, ask the person who has won a silver medal in the Olympics.

And to realize the value of time, in any increment, ask the person who spent twelve and a half years as a slave to drugs, followed by seven and a half years as an incarcerated felon.

Time is our most valuable commodity, bar none. It is, hands down, the most precious thing we have, yet it is the one thing with which we are most often wasteful. You can't recycle it, regain it, rejuvenate it, rediscover it, or reuse it. Once it's gone, it's gone. Now, I'm not saying we shouldn't have relaxation time, hobby time, lie-on-the–couch-and-read-a-book time, or sit-in-the–sun-and-do-absolutely-nothing time. It's all about balance in our lives. What I'm saying is that you need to respect and cherish your time as you would any precious gift and realize that every moment that you spend serving dead time is wasted.

Earlier in the book, I told you about my history with my ex-wife. Trust me, we had our fair share of differences over the years, as many couples who are no longer together have. I can't say that I even gave her the benefit of a simple divorce. I actually had the audacity to fight her for primary custody when I could barely even get myself out of bed in the morning. Throughout it all, however, we always had one thing in common: a great love for our son Eric.

I look back with astonishment at how lucky I was to be able to renew my relationship with my son. I've gone from being the type of dad who at times hardly remembered where I had last left his son to being the type of father that I think my dad and my granddad would be proud of. I think about that kid all of the time—mostly with pride, sometimes with worry, and always with love.

It may sound strange, but I think having to live in the prison environment for a portion of my life was a great advantage for me. I mostly kept my head down and tried to avoid any situation that seemed overly dangerous, but as I saw with Chuck in the story from the last chapter, it is not always possible to foresee a life-threatening situation. I learned never to take one second of my life for granted.

Upon my release, I wondered if I would retain that perspective. Perhaps it is because I had the lesson so vividly demonstrated for me in prison, but life in the outside world seems just as poignant.

A few years ago, my ex-wife Lisa and her husband Dave were driving down a dirt road in the Iowa countryside. Anyone who has been to Iowa knows that I have just described any one of about a thousand roads in the state. They were on this particular road because they were checking out an area they planned to visit later in the year for turkey hunting.

On their way out there, they saw a couple they were friends with but had not spoken to in a long time. They pulled over to chat with them and catch up a bit.

The couple raised horses and had several of them out in that area, both to give the animals exercise and to provide the couple with a change of scenery. They were far enough off the beaten path that there was almost never any traffic, and the closest thing resembling civilization was several miles off. In all, it made for a nice, peaceful afternoon.

Lisa's friend asked her if she had ever ridden, and Lisa replied that she had but not for many years. So her friend asked her if she would like to come with them for a ride and enjoy the scenery.

While this would have been an uncommon treat, Lisa turned it down, saying that she had come out with Dave that afternoon and that she should stay with him. But Dave told Lisa that she should take the opportunity and not worry about him; he would go scout the area and come back in a couple of hours to pick her up. It was settled—she would have a leisurely ride with her friend and he would see her when he got back.

Since Lisa wasn't an experienced rider, her friend decided to give her the horse that she had been riding for the past few hours. It was the most docile and a bit tired already, so it would be less inclined to get feisty with her.

They mounted their horses and began the peaceful ride down the road. Within minutes of beginning the ride, the horse that Lisa was on suddenly had an aneurism burst, reared up, and fell on Lisa, crushing her.

The nearest help was miles away. Their cell phones were out of range. The man with Lisa had to get in his car and drive just to get help. The paramedics assessed the situation and decided that Lisa was absolutely critical, so they called for a helicopter. In the meantime, Dave returned to the scene to find chaos. His wife lay there with blood coming from her eyes, nose, and ears.

From start to finish, Lisa clung to life for nearly three hours as they went for help, waited for the helicopter, and flew her to the hospital, where she died upon arrival. The couple informed Dave that she had only been on the horse for five minutes.

Lisa died in the prime of her life and left a son behind all because she was...

...on that particular road...

...on that particular day...

...meeting friends that she hadn't seen or talked to in years...

...who happened to talk her into riding the one horse that...

...despite having been ridden for hours already that day...

...had an aneurism that burst in that one moment...

. . . causing it to rear up and fall in just the right fashion . . .

. . . to end her life.

It gives you something to think about. How many of us, if hit by a bus tomorrow, could say that we had done everything in our power to live the lives we wanted? Would we go to our graves knowing that we had found that career, climbed that mountain, made time for our kids, or at least died trying? Or would we, instead, make a lot of excuses for why it had never been the perfect time to start?

Living a full life takes diligence. It takes a flat-out rejection of dead time. Remember those convicts I mentioned spending each and every day just like the one before it? Does that sound familiar? Waking up, walking like the living dead through yet another day at the office, grocery shopping, taking the kids to their games, making sure that you're home in time to cook dinner and watch the latest reality television show. If it does, you might not have committed a crime, but as sure as you're sitting there, reading this book today, you're doing dead time. It's easy to get in a rut, but it's also easy to get out of it. You just need a plan.

When I got out of prison, I had to come up with my own time management tool. What I needed was not a planner or PDA. I simply needed to give absolute priority to my goals. It was that easy. I gave myself short- and long-term goals that revolved around every facet of my life, not just my career. Once I reached one, I set another. Goals for my relationships, health, vacations, experiences, purchases, everything. Even now, throughout the day, just by habit, I ask myself, "Is what you're doing right now getting you any closer to those goals?" If the answer is no, I change what I'm doing. It's that simple. I never have to refill planner pages. I never lose my goals to a dead battery. They are with me twenty-four/seven, emblazoned on the chalkboard of my mind with great big priority exclamation marks next to them. I don't have to write them down. They're too important. How could I forget them? Writing something down means that you need a reminder, and needing a reminder means that you are not actively living your life.

I look back now at all of the time I wasted when drugs were the central focal point of my existence, and I look at the days I spent in prison becoming the person that I am today. If I had always known the value of time, what could I have accomplished? If I don't respect that time now, what will I miss?

Of course, everyone's goals and priorities are different, and yet I've found that too many people make their goals about the external things they want and tend to spend very little time on themselves when, in fact, the external goals mean nothing if you are not healthy in your mind, body, and soul.

I spent fourteen years destroying those things. I assigned no general importance to any of them, so that when I decided to turn my life around, I discovered that those three most basic parts of my existence had atrophied. My mind wasn't as sharp as it once was, I don't think I could have run from the cops even if I'd had the option, and my spirit was absolutely demolished. I couldn't even validate my existence.

In order to turn my life around, I had to start setting small goals just to get myself healthy enough to be able to concentrate on the greater goals of becoming whole again.

The first thing I had to do was clear my mind of the drugs. Then I gave myself the homework of researching scholarship programs and writing letters. It was rough at first, because it had been years since I had used my brain for anything other than figuring out how much I would need to steal to pay for drugs. After a while, all of the synapses were firing again, and I was eventually able to study for my degrees.

What I have since found, however, is that it can be just as easy to let your mind stagnate while living a normal life. Habits can be hard to break, and if your habit is to trudge through a day's work and then park your butt on the couch to watch television, your mind is serving dead time. The mind needs stimulation to stay sharp and I've learned to do my best to give mine what it needs.

While academics were my mind's main source of exercise while I was in prison, I've found that anything that stimulates you intellectually, expands your knowledge base, or offers a challenge between the ears is good mental exercise. Read a book. Write a book. Paint a picture. Take a cooking class. Research a topic you know nothing about. Build a model airplane using step-by-step instructions. Learn a new trade.

The activity may build toward an overall goal that you are working toward at the time, or it may just be an exercise to keep the brain agile for when you really need it. What's important here is that you chart new waters, challenge your mind, and explore new possibilities. If not stimulated the mind becomes stale, shuts down to the change around it, and serves as a hindrance to advancement and success. It is important to keep your mind sharp to prevent that from happening. They say idle hands are the devil's playground. I say an idle mind is an invitation for dead time.

Of course, it isn't enough just to get the engine running; you also have to ensure that the body and frame are equally up for the task. Once again, I had the challenge of removing the drugs from my system. I was malnourished, out of shape, and fighting to get the toxins out of my blood.

On the bright side, the one thing that prison does provide is an exercise yard, and I had a great deal of incentive to look as healthy and strong as I could. In prison, there are big fish and little fish and you don't want to look like easy pickings.

As I got healthier, I started to remember how it felt to have a healthy body. I found that not only was I moving better and feeling stronger, but I had the energy to get myself through each day, even the bad ones. I was assigning value to feeling healthy, and it made me want to work even harder at staying that way.

While your current goals may have nothing to do with your physiology, your overall health affects every part of your life. What I found was that hours of justification or self-loathing were never going to inspire me as much as a taste of good health. I just had to start feeling better and that fueled the fire. Better health makes life easier. It keeps you going when you have to work harder, it gives you the ability to handle stress better, and it opens up new possibilities for enjoying life. As an added benefit, it gets you up those stairs faster.

While jogging and weight-lifting were most accessible for me in prison and continue to be the staples of my workouts today, for you it could be yoga, climbing stairs, walking the dog, swimming, basketball, tennis, anything that leads to improving your physical well-being. It is not important what it is, only that we do it as a regular part of our schedule.

When I was in prison, exercise was factored into our everyday lives. It became a habit and that was the key! Today, I could no more miss my workout than I could miss breakfast or brushing my teeth before bed each evening. It is part of my daily routine and will become part of yours if you give it the chance to become a habit, a normal occurrence that requires no thought. Once it becomes second nature, you won't even have to talk yourself into it. It will even become another valued part of your day. I do my best thinking and come up with my best ideas while jogging. Some may find jogging to be boring, and prefer competitive sports. I have friends who enjoy the peacefulness of yoga. My parents like the intimacy of holding hands and walking each evening. The mode of exercise itself does not matter, only that we make the choice to do it.

You may feel like you are already in good physical condition, but dead time can find you here as well. Challenge yourself. Start somewhere, but as an activity becomes boring or easy, move onto something that pushes your limitations. Just as with the mind, the body is most easily improved when challenged. Try different activities, those you thought you would never be interested in or that you would be never be able to do. Later, when it comes time to meet an important deadline, win a race, or play with the grandkids, you will be ready.

While getting the mind and the body on the same page, you also have to address your soul. I am not going to subject you to any religious dogma; that is an individual choice and I will leave you to it. My advice is simply that you continually strive to find your way to your own peace, whether that's through organized religion, meditation, counseling, volunteerism, or just spending the day recognizing the little blessings that surround you. Your soul is your guide, the lodestar that leads you through life. You cannot enjoy a new job if your soul is ill at ease over the way you obtained it. You will not take pleasure in your new physique if you abused yourself to mold it. You will not cherish your success if you selfishly hoard it. In short, you cannot truly have any triumphs of the mind or body without your soul, so nurture it.

My sober soul was troubled by so many of the things I had done and the people I had harmed, and I had to find a way to make it whole again. I had to reach out to those I had hurt, while allowing them time to forgive. I had to create an idea of the man who I wanted to become—someone who I could not only live with, but be proud of. And, most importantly, I had to find a way to forgive myself so that I could move forward. When I had done those things, that's when I found peace. When I found peace, I finally started to hear the birds singing, and notice the leaves on the trees, and feel the acceptance and love of the family I had lost. I had not only started to see the successes in my life, but feel and enjoy them.

Think of these three areas as the necessities you want to have in your backpack as you travel your path. Once you have these three areas finely tuned and in perpetual motion, you will find that your goals come more and more easily and your path seems clearer than ever. You will be alert, spry, and at peace, and those are three very good things when you are on a journey. If you invest in yourself in these three areas, the rest of your goals will seem suddenly attainable, and you will know the satisfaction of never feeling remorse at the passage of time.

Chapter 12

Take the Key Away from the Guard

You are what you are and where you are because of what has gone into your mind, and you can change what you are and where you are by changing what goes into your mind.

—ZIG ZIGLAR

DIVINE INTERVENTION, KARMA, FATE—people have been naming the forces behind the paths we take for millennia. Like I said before, I am not here to argue religious dogma, but I do want to share some truths that I have gleaned from my life's experiences. They are based in faith: the faith that every person has a purpose and a potential that is waiting to be fulfilled and that we are rewarded or schooled based on the choices that we make along that path.

Think about all of the things that have happened in your life, the things that make up who you are today. Have you ever had anything go so exactly right that you could only explain it as luck? Did you take advantage of the luck in the best way possible, or did you waste it? Have you ever had something devastating happen to you that has made you ask "Why me?" Did you find an answer to that question? Did you try?

There is a series of children's books called "Choose Your Own Adventure." It takes the readers along a plot line and then, at a key point, asks them to make a crucial decision about what they would do. Once the readers make the decision, they turn to the page corresponding to that decision and learn their fate. That is kind of how I feel about life. There are numerous outcomes that are already written, but it is up to us to make the right choices.

Let's give it a shot.

You're Troy Evans.

You move to a new town and have the choice of toughing it out until you can make new friends on sports teams and in school, or you start doing bad things to make friends with the kids most available to you, even though you know what you're doing is wrong. You choose the bad kids, turn to that page of the book and discover, oh, bad luck, you become a drug addict.

You get married and have a kid. Do you choose to use your family's interventions to clean up your act and be a good husband and father, or do you choose drugs? Sorry, the drugs page says that your wife leaves you and takes your son with her.

Do you get sober, or rob banks to feed a habit? You choose to rob several banks in the hopes of either getting another fix or getting killed. Bad luck again; you're sent to jail to spend several years with yourself, thinking of every wrong that you've ever perpetrated against your family.

But here is where it gets interesting. The plot line can change as soon as you start making good decisions.

Once in jail, you choose sobriety over drugs, and gain clarity and a visit from your son, who shows you there is still hope.

You choose to fight to educate yourself rather than serving dead time, and are given a scholarship from the National Speakers Association that was never intended for someone like you.

You choose death over asking your family to smuggle drugs into prison for you, and the guards come in at just the right moment.

When all your hard work is snatched away from you, you choose to start over rather than returning to drugs and the life you fought your way out of, and you are told that you get to go home.

And my favorite: you choose a life of speaking to make a difference in other people's lives, and you find that you are given the unfettered opportunity to grow with them.

There is just too much coincidence. The more I think about it and the more I talk to others about their experiences, the more I am convinced that when you are choosing bad paths, you can get only bad, and when choosing good paths, good things are returned to you tenfold. How many sayings do we have about this exact same thing? You reap what you sow.... What goes around comes around....

Of course, it is important that you keep your eyes open, because the punishments do not always happen right away and the good things are not always delivered in the best packages. But once you start making the right decisions, even the past returning to haunt you can be turned into a blessing. I received one such lesson a relatively short time after being released from prison.

•

My first indication that something was wrong came as I opened the front door upon returning home from the office. The contents of our hallway closet completely littered the walkway in front of me. Upon entering the other rooms in the house I discovered every single drawer and cabinet in each room had been pulled out and upturned. We had been burglarized.

On that day, every single item of material value belonging to me and my wife of two months was taken: TV, VCR, stereo, computer, printer, fax machine, silver settings, and all of my wife's jewelry, including things that were handed down from her grandparents and her parents, things that could never be replaced. In addition to the monetary loss, every single room in our home was ransacked, and it would be days before our home resembled anything close to the home we knew. Was I angry? I was very angry. Did I want revenge? Of course I wanted revenge. I wanted more than anything to get my hands on those who had violated me, who had entered my space, who had taken from me.

Two days later, while sitting at my desk filling out insurance forms and compiling the list of what had been taken, I got to thinking about why it was that this had happened. And it slowly became apparent to me. I had never been on this end. I had never been the one who was violated, victimized, or stolen from. You see, it had always been me who was the taker, the thief, the one who victimized people. I had never known what it felt like to be the victim, to feel violated and taken advantage of. As I thought about this over the next several days I came to the conclusion that, like every other significant thing that had happened in my life, this too had a reason.

There was a purpose in this final leg of my transition, in which the robber became the victim. It emphasized the importance of my transformation. Slowly, I felt my anger dissipate, and a peace replaced it. I had to feel that pain to know in my heart that I would never cause anyone that kind of suffering again.

•

Have you ever noticed that some people are super lucky and others can't seem to catch a break? How much of that is perception? There are a lot of people who would have looked at the robbery as being terrible luck. That was my first reaction as well, but it goes back to that quote from the preface: *It is not important how we come to the events in our life. What is important is how we deal with those events.*

I believe that there is no such thing as luck; rather, the opportunities that are presented to you in life are a direct result of the way in which you walk through it. If, for example, you love yourself and are confident, people will see you as the type of person that they want to be around. On the contrary, if you are constantly negative and complaining, you will only attract other negative people. Who wants to spend the day with someone who will bring them down?

The same is true in the work place. If you demonstrate hard work and commitment, you will be rewarded. Who cares if you hate your job? Find a new one. But in the meantime, do the one you have to the best of your ability. Who knows, maybe your attitude will be noticed and a new job will find you.

I actually give a talk on this very issue to Human Resources professionals all of the time. I talk about how dead time is the greatest thief of productivity in the workforce today.

People complain about their jobs, bring their personal problems to work, and spend hours doing just about anything other than actually getting their work done. Then they will turn around and complain that their career is going nowhere. Honestly, what do they expect?

Then, when someone comes in with a go-getter attitude, the entire office turns on that person for being a tall poppy. How dare they come in and interrupt the status quo? When that person gets promoted over them, they will say it's because he or she's a suck-up and it isn't fair.

Could they possibly dig themselves any deeper into the world of the victim?

My point is this: If you are not actively making positive choices, you have no one to blame but yourself. Everything you do, from the way that you approach your job to the way that you operate in a relationship, to how you treat yourself on a daily basis and how you react to the things that happen to you, affects the results you will get out of life. The problem is that most people choose not to see the correlation.

If you don't like where your life is headed, try changing the little things first, and maybe the big things will follow. If something unfortunate happens, look for the lesson to be learned so that you can avoid having to learn it over and over again.

It is as simple as this: Good works produce rewards. If you put good out to the universe—good works, good choices, good vibes, whatever you want to call it—it will be returned to you. Have faith in that and you will not get lost.

Chapter 13

The Prosecution of Our Past

It's not what you are that holds you back, it's what you think you're not.

—DENIS WAITLEY

IT IS NOT IMPORTANT how we come to the events in our life. What is important is how we deal with those events. Or, as I like to call this chapter, "There is no such thing as a good excuse."

In this book, I have shared tales from my darkest hours as well as stories of my scholarships, reconciliation with my family, and full rehabilitation. I did not share them with you in order to brag. I told them to you hoping it would become clear that absolutely anything can be accomplished out here in the free world. If I could accomplish what I did within the harsh and violent confines of the federal prison, you can accomplish absolutely anything you want with all of the resources at your disposal.

In chapter one, I talked about that little voice, the one that tells you why you can't accomplish your goals. I talked about using hope to banish that voice, but now I'm going to give you the final blow, just in case you find that it's still hanging around. Are you ready? This is going to be pretty profound. Here it is:

That voice is a liar.

Listen to it for a second.... "You can't afford college." *Liar!* "You're too old to change your life." *Liar!* "You hit your wife because she deserves it." *Liar!* "You can't quit because your addiction is more potent than other people's." *Liar!*

How do I know the voice is lying? Because those are all excuses, and when it comes to what is best for you, there is no such thing as a good excuse. Can't afford college? Bull, I did it from prison. Too old? I've known older. Your wife deserves to be beaten? No one deserves that. You suffer from a super-potent mega-addiction? Mine made me stick a gun in the faces of innocent people and rob banks, and I kicked it.

I don't care what your background is, I don't care how you were raised, I don't care what ethnic group you belong to or creed you believe in, and I don't care what kind of bumps and bruises life has given you, or what potholes or obstacles it has thrown your way. You can accomplish absolutely anything you want to accomplish if you want it badly enough. Throw away the excuses and you will be set free to be the person you want to be. Cling to them and you will always fail for having never tried.

I heard this story while I was in prison and I want to share it with you. It's a story about two brothers whose lives were changed by the very same event, yet whose stories have very different outcomes.

In Australia, there is a story about two brothers caught stealing sheep. The penalty for the crime was fierce: a brand of the letters "ST" was seared onto each one's forehead, forever marking them as "Sheep Thieves."

For one brother the humiliation was overwhelming. Sneaking from town to town, he became crafty and cruel. Yet he never could get away from himself and finally died under suspicious circumstances after years of inner torment.

The other brother decided he had to face this crisis or be destroyed by it. He chose to earn back his self-respect. He began each day with the question "What can I do today to earn back my self-respect?"

As time went on, people began to trust him, and his past crime was forgotten. As he aged, he became a respected leader of the community, a friend to those who struggled, and an example of courage for the young.

Many years later a visitor came to town. He was surprised when he saw an old man shuffling past a storefront with the letters "ST" branded on his forehead. So he asked the clerk, "Who's that man? What's that all about?" The clerk said, "He used to be the mayor here. There was some story about how he got those scars on his forehead, but for the life of me I can't remember what it was. I think it had to do with him being a saint."

Drop the excuses. It is time for you to succeed.

PART FOUR

Q&A with an Ex-Con

Self is the only prison that can bind the soul.

—Henry Van Dyke

Chapter 14

Why Are You Talking to Me?

Destiny is no matter of chance. It is a matter of choice. It is not a thing to be waited for, it is a thing to be achieved.

—WILLIAM JENNINGS BRYAN

OKAY, SO THIS QUESTION is usually phrased "How did you get into public speaking?" Sometimes that is the question, pure and simple. However, different people ask the question for different reasons. For some, the underlying question is not just how I became a public speaker, but how I recovered from having screwed my life up so horribly. For others, the question is meant more as an accusation. Sort of a "Why are you getting paid for having been a blight on society?"

I have answers to all three.

I mentioned earlier that the first scholarship I received when I was trying to fund my education came from the National Speakers Association. While I was really more of a numbers kind of guy (I received my degrees in accounting and business), the thought on their part was that I would someday use my history to help others. I can't say, in all honesty, that I saw that as clearly as they did at first. I had screwed my life up so royally that I couldn't imagine anyone wanting to listen to me talk about it. I wasn't on the same page as they were, but I was very grateful for the money.

At first, I planned on taking just enough communication classes to keep them interested while I continued to look for additional sources of funding. But as I continued to correspond with my friend and mentor,

Robert Henry, and I saw the effect that I was having on my fellow prisoners, I started to see myself as they had seen me. People were noticing the things that I was doing, and the effect of it started to grow far beyond me and my own little cell. Gang members were looking for a future without violence, the educational programming was being expanded, and I even had a guard come up to me one day and tell me, "Evans, I told my son about you last night. He is living in the free world and not doing half of what you are doing with his life. You are a role model."

Of course, I walked you through the steps of my transformation in the earlier chapters as if my public speaking capabilities were always clear, but in reality, my purpose beyond becoming something better than I had been wasn't something I planned so much as a calling that was revealed to me. That was how I recovered so well and was able to make a full one-eighty. By the hand of God, Fate, Destiny, whatever you want to call it, I was put on a path. Once I saw the good that was coming from walking it, all of my doubts gave way to determination. My purpose became greater than I was, and that is what drives me today.

Of course, it's one thing to have an idea about what you want to do; it's another thing entirely to go and do it, especially if it's something that you've never done before. So how did I actually become a speaker?

Upon my release I met a man from the National Speakers Association who, as I mentioned earlier in the book, took me under his wing and gave me one of my first jobs. He was a speaker and author, and he was the one who mentored me in my speaking.

While my primary duties for him were administrative, my real job was to prepare myself for my new career. He helped me start to piece my message together and then made me go out every week to deliver it to whoever I could get to hear it—Kiwanis, Rotary Clubs, anyone who would give me a chance. In the beginning, I think those who had hearing aids that could be turned off liked my speeches the most.

I would videotape myself and bring it back for him to review. Every week, he would take the entire speech apart, piece by piece, telling me all of the things that I was doing wrong—I had the wrong cadence here, you could tell that I lost my train of thought there, I needed to pause a bit more, what was I doing with my hands. . . .

And then, like a father, he would build me back up so that I was prepared to go out and do it all over again. After a year of that, he told me I was ready to start my career and kicked me out.

Now that I am fortunate enough to be able to share my message with thousands of people each month, I find that there will always be those who are mad at me for making a living off my story.

All I can say to those people is... I feel blessed each day to be able to be paid for doing something that is so much a part of my heart, what I feel to be my true calling. I have paid my debt to society and rebuilt myself into a successful, upstanding citizen. The slope of my downfall was steep and slippery and I worked very hard to climb my way back up. I'm proud of that, and in the end, helping just one other person do the same would far outweigh any criticism that you could give me.

While some people focus on what they perceive to be the fair or unfair in this world, I also have files full of letters and e-mails from the people whose lives I have touched. For me, the true payment is in the note from the kid who says that I have helped him put down the joints and refocus on education, the parent who says that I have helped her break down the barriers that stood between her and her child, or the people who have used my words to make a change in their lives.

If that's still not enough for you, then know that I am also using my success to touch the lives of kids who have lost their way. Each year, I donate my time and my message to kids who have found themselves in trouble with the law. Believe it or not, these are the hardest speaking engagements I've been rewarded with so far. It's not easy to gain access to any correctional facility once you've been a convict. It's taken sorting through miles of red tape for the corrections department just to let me inside the building. But I feel that it's my duty to those kids and to society.

I am still, to this day, trying to create the same inroads with the adult prison system. For good reason, they have rules against letting ex-cons into the prisons to meet with the other prisoners. However, I continue to try to change their minds in this one instance. I can pinpoint the precise day that I first chose the easy path and changed my life forever. Many of those people can as well, and live with the regret just as I do. I want to help them see a future beyond that.

Of course, there are those who, like my old warden and the people who stand up in the crowd and tell me that I have no right to be living my life the way I do, will say that a prisoner's place will always be in the prisons or the ghettos of our country.

I've found from talking to many of them that, as the saying goes, while they point their fingers at me, they are pointing three back at themselves. It is my job to take my listeners outside of their comfort level, and not everyone likes what they see once they're there.

If you're one of those people, let me ask you this: Why is it so important to *you* that I pay for my mistakes for the rest of my life? I guarantee you that if you really search your soul, it has nothing to do with me.

Chapter 15

Who Needs to Change?

The whole point of being alive is to evolve into the complete person you were intended to be.

—OPRAH WINFREY

WHO NEEDS TO CHANGE? Anyone who is not perfect, and that absolutely includes me.

I have an extreme story. My history is uncommon and I've been to a lot of places in my life that I wouldn't wish on anyone.

From the standpoint of a speaker who is trying to help others affect change in their own lives, this can be a blessing and a curse. Obviously, for those who need to make some serious changes in their own lives, a parallel might be easily drawn. I am thankful each and every day for being able to touch the lives of those people.

On the other hand, there are many people who are going through life without addiction, tragedy, financial struggles, etc. In fact, if someone were to ask us how we were doing, we would inevitably tell them that we were... wait for it... "fine."

I am no longer addicted to drugs. I don't rob banks, either. I am an upstanding member of society. I make a good living. I have a family that loves me. There are millions of people in this world who would trade places with me in a heartbeat.

And yet there is always room for improvement. To illustrate, let me give you this example.

I am not perfect. Let me tell you why that's a problem in my life.

I've just laid bare my entire history, and I do that on a daily basis. That is my sales pitch when I'm trying to get myself hired. I tell people what a fantastically, diabolically, heart-breakingly dishonest blight on society I was. Then, I turn around and ask them to enter into a business agreement with me and trust me with their deposit, to show up, show up sober, and not rob their audience once I get there.

Is that what they're thinking? I know for a fact, sometimes, that it is. And so, in my mind, I've decided that the only way to counterbalance that is to be perfect. Perfectly on time, perfectly precise in my accounting, perfectly precise in my agreements, perfectly clear in my communication, perfectly open with references, and perfectly entertaining when I come to do an event.

I am hyper-diligent at the expense of my sanity, my time with my family, and my own peace of mind. When I do make a mistake, which happens on occasion despite my best efforts, I crawl into my head and stay there poking around at all of the coulda-shoulda-wouldas that I can possibly find and don't come out for a long, long time.

As if that wasn't enough of an issue, I believe that everyone else should be perfect as well. I went through a period in my life where my word meant nothing to anyone, including myself. I continue to feel the stigma of that loss to this day. And yet, in this day and age, so many people fling their words around as if they were inconsequential. They don't think twice about being late for no good reason, playing the office blame-shifting game, or telling "harmless" little white lies.

While I do believe that people should be more diligent in guarding their words, the problem arises when I become so hypersensitive that I forget that sometimes being late can truly be an unforeseeable, unintentional accident.

That is something that I am working on.

My point in sharing this is that I did not write this book to present myself as perfect or the end result of having "fixed" myself. There will always be change and there will always be things in my life that can be improved upon. The process and the path never end, and they can help you change far more than the large and daunting problems in your life.

What I invite you to do is see the journey that is waiting for you in even the little things you would like to improve. Make more money, spend more time with your friends, take a class in Spanish, cooking, comedic improvisation, whatever; there is always room for improvement and dead time beckons to the stagnant.

Chapter 16

Why Was I Given This Book?

If you have a good friend, you don't need a mirror.

—GERMAN PROVERB

IF YOU'VE BEEN WANTING to make a life change, chances are you were given this book by a good friend to help you take those first steps. If that is the case, I hope this book helps and I'm glad I've been able to touch your life in some small way.

If you haven't been planning any sort of life change and you can't imagine why you've received this book, then it is probably because someone who loves you, likes you, doesn't like you so much, or works with you thinks you need to rethink your situation. Maybe they even just left it on your doorstep in a clear attempt at literary ambush.

To you I say this: It might be worth taking the suggestion. It is all too common for people to only see the things they want to see, and at times it can be hard to look at the larger picture.

When I was just a few years into my prison sentence, just starting to get on a roll with my education, we had an incident in the prison.

I'm not sure exactly how it started, but for some reason, a couple of members of the Mexican Mafia had a beef with one of the members of one of the black gangs (I don't remember if it was the Bloods or the Crips, and frankly it doesn't matter). These two guys in the Mexican Mafia jumped the other gang member and did some pretty good damage before they were broken up. A couple of days later there was a retaliation and a member of the Mexican Mafia went down.

Racial tensions were out of control and everyone was on guard for signs of trouble. It was no longer enough to simply make sure you didn't tick anyone off. Now there was the chance that you would become involved in something just by being in the wrong place at the wrong time. Things were bad.

A couple of days went by, and the heightened stress levels had raised the stakes even higher. After lunch, about seventy-five guys actually rose up against the guards and started pelting them with rocks and swinging broom sticks at them. It was an impromptu act that had very little planning behind it, and the guards quickly broke it up.

The prison was put in a low-grade lockdown. We were still able to go to our shift jobs, but for the most part, we were stuck in our cells for a few days. The hope was that this would be enough to calm the tension inside the prison. When they released us to normal status just a couple of days later, however, it seemed that all they had done was provide some of the inmates with the time they needed to plan.

This time it wasn't seventy-five, but nearly 300 inmates who surged up. It started in the recreation yard and quickly spilled inside the prison walls. Within each bunkhouse of that particular institution, there were escape doors inside the guard's office. When the guards fear for their lives, they are supposed to seal the office and use the escape doors to make it to safety. We weren't supposed to know about the doors, but just try to keep a secret like that from the people who are looking for any and all ways out. The prisoners were going for the doors.

In the end, none of them made it out a door, but neither did one of the female corrections officers. Now the stakes were even higher. As you might imagine, they roughed her up pretty good. A few of the guys wanted to rape her, as well, and it was only thanks to the intervention of some of the prisoners that she wasn't ravaged on the spot. For the time being, she was alive and intact. But if we thought there was going to be a problem before, now we were sure of it. Now there was a hostage.

For a day and a half, the prisoners held the prison. During that time, I stayed tucked away in my cell or an office trying not to draw any attention to myself. I just hunkered down and prayed that the situation wasn't going to end as badly as I anticipated. The actions of the rest of the population varied. There were those who, like me, just wanted to stay away from it all. There were others who took part in some of the looting and enjoyed other small bits of freedom that they might not otherwise have had, such as more television time, days off from their prison jobs, etc. And then there was the fraction of the population that had started the entire thing. They were running rampant, usually without purpose, with no way out, causing nothing but violence and destruction.

In the meantime, through the few small windows to the outside, we could see every state and federal law enforcement agency they could assemble preparing. They set up a manned perimeter around the prison. Guards and police officers were armed with M-16s and shotguns and told to shoot anyone trying to make a break for it. Command posts were set up and a special prison task force was brought in.

On day two, they were ready to take back the prison. They rolled an armored vehicle into the yard and literally smashed it right into one of the buildings (the one where the female guard was being held). That was the first section of the prison they took back.

A storm of armed officers began to sweep through the prison. Tear gas was released into the ventilation system, and suddenly anyone who was inside the prison was on the floor just trying to breathe. The officers swept from room to room, beating anyone they encountered into submission regardless of what they were doing and handcuffing them to whatever was close by and immoveable.

If you were lucky enough or smart enough to be in your own cell when the breach occurred, you were able to escape with nothing but the effects of the tear gas. Our doors were simply shut, and frankly, it was the first time I had felt safe in two days. If, however, you had the misfortune of being one of the people who had decided not to participate in the riot but to still take advantage of the extra television time, then you were beaten down and handcuffed wherever they found you. Anyone suspected of being involved was basically hogtied and dragged out into the yard for questioning and subsequent punishment.

It took a day and a half for the guards to take back control of the entire prison, but we all paid for it for years. We soon found our lives even more restricted than they had been before, of course, but the truly long-term punishments were perpetrated by our fellow inmates.

I mentioned earlier that FCI Florence was a new prison. Some of the benefits of that were a beautiful gymnasium with a basketball court for use during the winter months, a law library, and a GED program with on-site classrooms.

Frustrated by their failed attempt at a break, the rioting inmates had turned on the prison itself. They went into these areas and absolutely destroyed them. They broke windows, trashed computers, and set fire to anything that would burn. As a result, the sprinkler system came on, destroying anything the prisoners hadn't, right down to the floorboards of our basketball court. As you can imagine, there was no hurry to replace these things. There was no basketball, no library, no classes; the whole place was just trashed.

So you might be saying, "Gee Troy, that was a fascinating peek inside a prison uprising, but what does that have to do with me or why I have this book?"

Here it is:

1. You cannot change a problem if you refuse to see it.
2. Ignoring it will not make it better and will probably make it worse.
3. In the absence of a true solution, we will often turn destructively in on ourselves.
4. We will generally take those around us down, too.

There were quite a few conversations once order was restored about what had gone wrong. The media speculated about the nature of the caged animal, and the prison found a few scapegoats and acted like they were making the modifications necessary to prevent it from happening again, but inside, the prisoners were all saying the same thing: "They should have seen it coming a mile away."

The signs were all there; they just didn't want to see what was right in front of their faces. Those of us who could smell it in the air had already started to venture out a little less, take a little more stock of who was around us, and stop blinking days before anything happened. They should have seen it coming.

Perhaps you've received this book because those around you see your situation with more clarity than you see it yourself. I know that that was the case with my addiction. My family always knew how much trouble I was in even when I thought I had them completely snowed. They were trying to take my blinders off with intervention after intervention, and I was so convinced by my own lies that I couldn't do it. I didn't want to deal with the problem.

So let me just tell you this: If someone gave you this book, you're not fooling anyone. You have a problem and they're trying to tell you something. It may not be drugs. It could be an emotional issue, a marriage on the rocks, a job in peril. If you look deep down I'm sure you know what they're trying to tell you. My advice is to face it and get on the path to change today. This could be your pivotal point.

Chapter 17

How Do I Change the Unchangeable?

Change your thoughts and you change your world.

—NORMAN VINCENT PEALE

THERE IS NO SUCH THING as an unchangeable situation. If there is one message that you should take with you from this book, that is it.

Over the years, I have had the benefit of meeting thousands of people. Everyone has their own story. Some people have experienced personal tragedies, some are in situations that seem impossible to escape, and still others have become so bogged down in their lives that they don't even know how to take a first step anymore.

When these people ask for advice, I tell them that there is one thing that can always be changed: their attitude. If you tell yourself that there is no way out of a situation over and over again, then you'll be right. You can go through life dwelling on all the reasons that things will never change. You can lay the reasons out one after the other, point to each of them and say, "See, I told you so." In reality, however, all you've done is point out the excuses you've used to build yourself your own internal prison.

I can feel the argument boiling up inside some of my readers. The "you don't understand"s and the "you're oversimplifying the situation"s are already perched indignantly on their lips, ready to spring forth. And yet I say, you can always change your attitude.

We all have things in our lives that we cannot change. We can't, for example, change the death of a loved one, things that happened to us when we were younger, or the fact that a spouse has left us. But remember what I said in the preface of this book: *It is not important how we come to the events in our life. What is important is how we deal with those events.*

If you are going through life in misery, or things haven't turned out the way you planned and you're stuck in your own existence, you have only one person to blame—yourself. Sadly, we're often so busy pointing our fingers at other people and circumstances that we don't realize that each time we do, we are giving our power away. Every time you make an excuse that makes you the victim, you are taking away any chance you have of making yourself whole again.

When I first started using drugs, my father was furious. He tried grounding me, locking me out of the house, threatening my freedom; in short, everything he could think of to make me do what was right. He had been raised on a farm with a good work ethic and a strong sense of family obligation and morality. In his eyes, everything I was doing was flying in the face of what should be done. Meanwhile, he was quickly exhausting the list of things that he felt could be done to turn me around.

As far as he was concerned, he had raised me "right." He had shown me discipline and role-modeled strength and responsibility, and it was just unbelievable to him that he had this son who couldn't seem to do right even once in a while just by accident. He was doomed to being the guy with the drug-addicted son.

As I said before, my family did manage a few interventions during my drug-using days. On one such occasion, they managed to get me into a fantastic and very expensive program at a place called Cottonwood Hills. It was a thirty-day in-patient treatment program that started with five to six days of detox, took us through the usual twelve steps, and then ended with what they called family week.

During that week, we first went to speak to families of other members of the treatment program. This was meant to show that none of us were alone in our problems and that drugs affected people from all walks of life.

After that, we had to deal with our own families through a variety of exercises. For the first time in a while, my father and I were forced to talk to each other. They gave us a series of exercises to do.

The first exercise required us to tell each other what we were angry about. We each had a very long list, mine about our move and his about my drug use and disrespect.

Next, we each had to come up with a list of things that we didn't like about the other person. That was easy. We had been doing that for years, and honestly, we probably each could have gone on all day long with this assignment, each of us was so angry with the other.

In the next exercise, however, we had to write down a list of things that we liked about each other. I managed to write down two or three things. My father came back to the room with one. We had been adversaries for so long at this point that we couldn't even remember the days when I was younger and we were best buddies. We couldn't remember the days at the ball fields or the hunting trips or the talks around the dinner table. We were both so invested in being angry at one another that we had lost the foundation for having any other kind of relationship.

At that point, the counselor sent us back to our tables and told us that we were not going to be able to finish the assignment until we had at least half as many good things to say about each other as we had bad. He told us that he didn't care if it was something that we felt now or in the past or even if we had to make it up. The next time we came together, we were going to say only nice things to each other.

Talk about changing perspective. Once we stopped resisting the process, you could see us both releasing our aggressive postures. We were meeting each other with kindness rather than accusations for the first time in years. We were changing our attitudes toward one another, letting go of our adversarial roles, and remembering that we were family members who loved one another deep down. That would never change.

The last exercise we were assigned was to each tell the other person what we felt we could have done differently and what parts of the past we each took responsibility for.

My part was easy. I was a drug addict who had thrown my life away. I knew it, he knew it, and our neighborhood knew it. I had been expecting that part of the session and it came to me almost by rote.

But then it was my dad's turn and I got the surprise of my life. The last exercise had opened his eyes to me again for the first time in years. It had let him see me as the son who had looked to him for love and guidance. I was expecting to hear him tell me that it was all my fault and that he did everything that he could. That is what I had heard for years. Instead he started to cry and told me he was sorry.

He was sorry for not knowing better how to help me through my problems. He was sorry for taking such a hard-handed approach to parenting instead of realizing that it wasn't working and changing his ways back then. He was sorry for uprooting the entire family and turning a deaf ear to my cries for help. He was sorry for the role that he had played in allowing his little boy to turn into a drug addict with nothing to live for.

On that day, the unchangeable was changed. I wish that I could say that I walked out of that clinic a drug-free man for life, but you already know that that's not true. What did change was my relationship with my father. We hugged that day for the first time in years. We allowed ourselves to love each other and remember what it had been like when I was a boy. We both had been living without that feeling for so long, and yet there it was; it had been there the entire time. That day might not have been the ultimate solution, but we both left that session with the feeling that a hole had been filled. We were more complete than we had been when we came. We found out that there was something more important than being right or winning the argument. It didn't matter who had done what to whom as long as he was still my father and I was still his son.

That was the day we laid the first pieces of the foundation from which we have been able to build a fantastic relationship. If we had never taken the opportunity to change our attitudes, even if only under duress, we might never have known again what it feels like to be father and son. Our only regret is that we didn't change sooner. It might have made all the difference in my world.

•

On the day I just described, my father and I had one thing in common: we thought that our relationship was irreparable and lost forever. Yet in one exercise, that counselor was able to completely change our perceptions. We were so caught up in the futility of the situation and in our own anger that it never even occurred to us that we could simply change our minds and operate out of forgiveness and love by opening our hearts to one another again. The answer to the unanswerable, the change in the unchangeable, was that simple.

What I'm asking you to consider is that, perhaps, there *is* a way to change your situation. Perhaps there is a solution to the problems that you perceive to be insurmountable, and all you have to do to find it is to believe that it exists.

Change your perspective. Stop looking at your situation from the negative and start taking steps toward the positive. Choose not to lose your future to self-pity or despair and make up your mind right now that things can be different.

I told you before about my relationship with my son while I was in prison. I met many people inside who had given up their relationships as soon as they went in. They were so ashamed that they denied their children the sight of them, their correspondence, their rights to a father.

As I said, I had a different attitude. If I was going to be in prison for more than a decade, I was going to be the best prison dad possible. In fact, I was probably being the best dad that Eric had ever known because, for the first time in his life, he didn't have to talk to me through a haze of drugs. He had my undivided attention when we were together and he received a letter from me every single day of my incarceration.

I told you about my friend Jack earlier, the high-school buddy of mine who freaked out at the quarry and ran into the woods for hours because he was so high on acid that he didn't know what was reality and what was hallucination anymore. He could have let drugs beat him like they did the rest of us in the group. Instead, he started doing drywall, built a small business for himself, grew it into a large business, and now owns a horse ranch in Colorado.

I had another friend inside who had descended so far into the world of crime that when the police came to raid his house for the drugs and weapons stashed inside, he actually shot at the police helicopter and tried to bring it down. As you can imagine, he was given a substantially longer prison term than my own. He not only earned his bachelor's, but also went on to obtain a master's and is now a manager at a car dealership.

There are endless stories that go the same way. There is no such thing as a situation that cannot be changed.

I can't tell you what the solution to your problem is, but I can tell you that there is one. I also speak from experience when I say that people who climb out of the victim role and start taking accountability for where they are in their lives and where they are going tend to make their own luck. The moment that I made the decision to put down the excuses and take responsibility for my lot in life, good things started happening to me. Call it Karma or the hand of God; call it whatever you want. As far as I'm concerned, it happens too often to be coincidence.

Chapter 18

What Advice Do You Have for Parents?

The best inheritance a parent can give to his children is a few minutes of their time each day.

—M. GRUNDLER

EVERY TIME I FINISH one of my presentations I am greeted by a sea of parents. Most of them are in search of the keys to keeping their children away from drugs and out of trouble. The remaining few don't even need to speak. I see the looks on their faces and know that they are the same looks my parents wore so many years ago. They are wondering if it is already too late.

My advice to all of them is always the same—keep an open line of communication by any means possible, make sure your kids are fully educated, and beware of the "have to" mentality that can keep you from making the best decision for your child.

What does all that mean?

Let me tell you what not to do. Don't wait until you find a joint in your kid's bedroom and then say, "Smoking this stuff will make you stupid. You're grounded."

Start talking to your kids about drugs early and often. I mean really early. Kids these days are exposed to drugs at a shockingly young age.

In my role as speaker, I have had the benefit of becoming involved with a program called DrugTalk.org. Their Web site reveals that current estimates place 84 percent of families with children at a moderate-to-high risk of drugs. And while many parents think that their children are learning enough from the barrage of anti-drug campaigns that they see on television and hear at school, DrugTalk.org cites studies that point to one conclusive fact—nothing, including these multi-million dollar campaigns, has anywhere near the effectiveness of parental involvement through open communication.

I would advise any parent to go to the site. It has a great deal of useful information and tools for both you and your kids to maintain an open dialogue about drugs.

If they don't hear these things from you, they will get their "information" from their peers. If that peer is trying to get them to do the drug, I can guarantee you that it won't be accurate.

When I was being lured into the drug world, I heard it all: "You can't get hooked from doing it once." "Marijuana is harmless." "Everyone smokes pot."

Once I bought into that sales pitch and became hooked myself, I started spinning it back out to the newbies with just as much certitude. There I was, hooked on the stuff, screwing my life up and telling my fellow classmates, my girlfriend, and my friends that drugs were completely safe and you couldn't get hooked.

This information is too important to trust to anyone else. Make the time to research the current drug trends, stay current on drug terminology, and provide your kids with the absolute hard truth about what drugs will do to you. Don't sugarcoat it. Show them how a pot smoker's brain waves are changed by minimal use, show them pictures of meth users who have gaping wounds they've inflicted on themselves because they thought there were bugs under their skin, show them the news reports of kids who will be in jail for the rest of their lives because they drank or used drugs and then drove. In short, show them the consequences of making the wrong choices in the most vivid detail that you can. Scare the pants off them so that the decision is a no-brainer, and keep talking to them so that the message stays loud and clear.

Once you've armed them with information, help give them the tools that they'll need to battle peer pressure. They need to have a response ready so they can send a clear message when they are offered drugs. This will differ from kid to kid. Some will feel completely confident telling their classmates that they think that drugs are about the dumbest choice that you can possibly make. For others, sometimes it's nice to have parents for scapegoats—"No way. My parents study this stuff in their sleep and wait up for me. I'd be busted as soon as I walked through the door."

Next, make sure that the line of communication goes both ways. From the time that your kids are young, make a point of talking to them about their day. Know who their friends are, what they're doing, and whose parents are good supervisors. If your kids are used to an open line of communication, they'll be more inclined to share things with you as they get older, and if they stop, you'll have a warning sign.

Earlier in this book, I talked about conversations around the family dinner table. When I started to withdraw from our nightly conversations, you can bet my parents' ears perked up.

"Where did you go?"

"Nowhere."

"What did you do?"

"Nothing."

"Who were you with?"

"Nobody."

Maybe you remember that conversation from your own teenage years. If you're like most of the teens who have engaged in that dialogue, you know that if you weren't forthcoming with the details, there was usually a good reason.

If you're on the parental side of the conversation, it is your cue to find new ways of getting your kids to open up. It won't necessarily be easy. Your kids will accuse you of prying into their business, not trusting them, etc. In truth, they might never have given you a reason not to trust them. However, if their behavior is becoming more secretive, and if they feel like they can't let you in on some part of their lives, you owe it to your child to not take the easy path, but rather keep communicating until you know that your child has the tools that he or she needs to be safe.

That brings me to one of the most unpopular suggestions I give to parents—give your kid a guarantee that they can tell you anything without being punished. You heard me: no yelling and screaming, no grounding, no taking the car away, no punishment.

Trust me, as a parent, I know this can be a difficult pill to have to swallow. You may end up hearing things you never wanted to hear: teenage sex, drinking, drugs, underage driving. Be prepared for the worst—the rule still applies.

Does that mean you can't be mad? No way. I can tell you I've had to leave the room once or twice to cool down before continuing a conversation with my own son. But the important thing is that he feels like he can come to me with anything.

Not only do parents need to make this guarantee, but they need to acknowledge that there is no such thing as a "bad time" to talk when their child is in trouble. When your kids start talking, everything else in the world has to cease to exist. You have to be willing to put aside any distractions and be completely in that moment with your children. If they are opening up to you, your reaction will speak volumes. It will shape their perception of what their value is to you, whether your love is unconditional or may be withheld, and also whether you were being truthful with them when you said they could come to you with anything.

It is not enough just to make the deal. You have to follow through with it and make that moment the most important moment of your life. Your children should be treated to nothing less.

I can't tell you how many times, when I was first spinning out of control, I would have loved to have felt like I could come to my family for help getting on the right path. I was trying to be noticed. I was trying to hit my father's radar in some way, and I was utterly screwing up my life in the process.

Of course, in those days, the general rule of parenting was to rule with a stern hand and make the punishment suit the crime. I don't fault them for raising me in the same fashion that they had been raised. On the other hand, I had a choice and a unique perspective to take into consideration when it came time for me to start parenting my own child. Just because that had been the way for generations did not mean that it was the best way.

Will there be times when you want to ground your children until they're able to file for social security? You bet. But there will be moments in their lives when they don't need the firm hand of discipline so much as guidance and the knowledge that you will always love them. Don't fail them. That could be their pivotal point.

My final words of advice on the subject are watch out for the "have to mentality" that might be keeping you from making the right decisions for your family.

What is the "have to" mentality? It is the assumption that you have no choice but to make the decision that you are making regardless of the results. It is what lets you stop looking for a better solution and accept the conventional wisdom.

Let me spell it out for you: If you have a child who you feel is in real danger of falling into the world of drugs, crime, etc., nothing should be more important in your life than finding an alternative that helps to protect him or her.

I find that sometimes parents are so focused on the things they think that they "have to do" or "can't do" that they lose sight of the things that they absolutely need to do. It usually sounds something like . . .

"Can we discuss this later? I have to go to work."

"I know that my kid is hanging out with the wrong crowd, but I can't just move, take him out of his school, monitor his every move, etc."

"I can't take time off from work."

"I know it means more time away, but I have to take this promotion."

It is not hard to get caught up in our lives, our careers, and the "have to" aspect of our daily routines, and lose sight of the things that are truly important. Moreover, it is easy to let an "I can't" be an excuse to drop the ball entirely.

Here is my point: Would you rather be late to work or take a sick day and know that you were there to hear your child's cry for help, or have a spotless attendance record?

Would you rather stay in a neighborhood or town where your child's access to drugs is uninhibited just because it makes your commute a little easier, or find a better environment and drive an extra fifteen minutes every morning? (Don't fool yourself, a wealthy neighborhood can be just as dangerous as the ghetto when it comes to access to drugs.)

Would your promotion be as sweet if you knew that it was at the expense of your child's well-being?

Now let's deal with the "can't" issues. Maybe you feel that you truly cannot miss a day of work or move. First, are you absolutely sure? Okay. If you are, then what are your other options? Who else might be able to help you reach your child? A mother, sibling, aunt, uncle, minister, teacher? How can you make more time to spend with your child when you are not at work?

The point is, don't assume that a "have to" is truly a "have to" and a "can't" means that you have no options. It might mean making sacrifices, calling in favors, moving to a smaller, less expensive house, or sacrificing a career move, but that's the job you took when you had a child. If there is a choice, I urge you not to let your regrets fall on the side of your child.

Chapter 19

You're as Old as My Mom and Dad. What Do You Know?

You must learn from the mistakes of others. You can't possibly live long enough to make them all yourself.

—SAM LEVENSON

WHAT I KNOW IS THAT, when I was your age, I made a lot of mistakes.

I am about to lay some of the incidents of my teenage years out for you to see in detail and I'm going to tell you exactly how I felt back then. I want you to read my story carefully, because more than likely, you will face some or all of the same decisions that I had to make at some point in your life. I am asking that you learn from my mistakes so that you don't have to suffer the consequences of making them yourself.

I mentioned briefly before that I moved to a new town and a new school the summer before I started high school. I had to leave my friends behind. The life that I knew and everything that I was were gone. I had to start over from scratch. Let me tell you something—I was ticked. Actually, I was so much more than ticked, but I'm not sure that a G-rated term for how angry I really felt exists. It felt like the whole world was against me, and my parents didn't seem to care if they ruined my life or not. From what I could see, all they were worried about was my father's new promotion and making sure the family didn't embarrass him.

When I complained about the move, their response was that I should go and make new friends, so that's exactly what I did. School was out, so I made friends with the kids in my neighborhood. I was especially drawn to one group because they hung out with a girl who was gorgeous and an athlete like me.

She played soccer and was the top scorer in her summer league. She was smart. Just to add a little intrigue to the situation, I found out that she had an older brother who was a drug dealer and that she herself had the dark little secret of occasional drug use. She would smoke pot on the weekends and sometimes at night.

In short, she was not only good-looking, but she was exactly who I wanted to become in this new town. She was an athlete who made good grades, and she was accepted by just about every clique in the school. She could hang out with the jocks, talk books with the nerds, was beautiful enough to be a cheerleader, and had an edge that let her fit in with the stoners. If I was the newbie outcast, she was the exact opposite of that. When she agreed to go out with me, it was the best thing that had happened to me since we had packed our bags in Phoenix.

The first time she offered me a joint, I barely hesitated to take it. There were so many reasons I could think of for not turning her down. I didn't want to seem like I wasn't cool. It seemed as if I were the only one who hadn't smoked pot before, and I didn't want to stand out. I had heard all of the "don't do drugs" campaigns before, and yet here was this wonderful girl who did do drugs and seemed to be highly successful. If she could do it, why couldn't I? Most of all, I had just found a group of friends and a new girlfriend. I wasn't alone in a new town anymore. I was part of something, and I didn't want to screw that up. In the end, they barely had to say a word. I was going to smoke pot because they did it; that was a good enough reason for me.

In truth, I didn't know a thing about it. I knew that my dad had told me it would make me a deadbeat, but that seemed to be such a general statement, and I thought I was seeing proof to the contrary in my girlfriend. I didn't know how wrong I was.

As I said, my girlfriend's brother was a dealer and he kept his sister well-supplied. She would share her drugs with me, or I would take a hit or two from some of the other people in the group, but after a while, that just made me a mooch. My friends were happy to give me enough to get me hooked, but their generosity quickly came to an end. I was going to have to start buying my own pot and that meant I needed to come up with the money to do it.

At first I was able to con the money out of my parents, but it didn't take them long to figure out what was going on. They started trying to intervene, but that just made me more angry with them. I remember thinking that they were only upset because they didn't have the perfect little family anymore and it might make Dad look bad. Then I thought, *Good, it's his fault anyway. If we hadn't moved, none of this would be happening.* Every time they yelled at me or grounded me, it just made me angrier at them, and I would push the envelope just a little further.

It didn't take long before I was trying more than just pot: cocaine, acid, you name it. If it was around back then, I was trying it out. I knew that it was wrong, and yet I still did it. I figured that pot didn't seem to be as bad as my parents had said, so maybe cocaine wasn't that bad either, or acid, or mushrooms. I kept telling myself that none of these drugs seemed as bad as my parents had made them sound, but all the while, I had started failing classes, been kicked off my sports team, and was in trouble with my parents all the time.

I was taking risks with more than just drugs, too. By that time, I had talked my girlfriend into experimenting with some harder drugs as well. She was losing her edge athletically and we were throwing caution to the wind in just about every area of our lives.

Not only had we started having sex, but since we both had basement bedrooms with windows that opened, I had started sneaking over to her house to spend the night. I would creep into her room late at night, stay there until four in the morning, and then return home.

One night, we forgot to set the alarm clock and fell asleep. When we woke up, everyone in the house was already awake as well. We were whispering back and forth, trying to decide what to do, when her mother heard voices. We could hear her coming down the stairs asking who was in the room. It was all I could do to throw my naked body under the bed while her mother banged on the locked door and my girlfriend rushed to put clothes on, all the while telling her mom that she had heard the radio.

I watched as her mother's feet circled the bed, stopping first at the closet, then swinging the door open to check that I wasn't hiding behind it. It wasn't long before I saw her drop to her knees and peer under the bed. She barely had time to tell me to get out from under the bed and begin calling for her husband; I grabbed a sheet off the bed as my only cover, jumped out the window, and ran past all of our neighbors, who were retrieving their morning papers or mowing their lawns and could see exactly what was going on.

When I got home, my dad had locked me out of the house for sneaking out once again. I banged on the door, and as he opened it for me, surveying me and my sheet, he shook his head and said, “Now you’ve really gone and done it, haven’t you?”

Moments later, the phone rang and my dad came into the room. He told me that my girlfriend’s father had just called and that I was to go back there immediately. I told him there was no way I was going back there, to which my dad replied, “If you’re going to act like a man, you need to go down there and take responsibility for your actions like a man.” And with that, he sent me back down there on my own to face her father.

There I sat in front of a Marine General who kept swords as wall decorations. Any one of those blades was within a moment’s grasp and he was telling me about how he was going to kick my head in and bury me in the wilderness if I ever so much as touched his daughter again. I had never been so scared in my entire life.

Three months later, I got his daughter pregnant. She was absolutely torn up by the decision to have an abortion. She had to pick up the emotional tab for that and left for the procedure a wreck. My main concern was that I had to use the money I had been saving for a car to pay for it.

Of course you can tell that her father didn’t follow through on his threats, although I am certain that he wanted to several times over the next few years. My girlfriend was sixteen when she had her first abortion. Even then, our parents couldn’t keep us apart, and we were too dumb to know just how much we were screwing up our lives. All we knew was that we were “in love” and that nothing could come between us.

I was a year older than her and made it out of high school by the skin of my teeth. By the time her senior year came around, any thoughts of athletic or academic scholarships had long left her dreams as well.

She was about to enter adult life and had even fewer coping skills than I had. By that time, I had graduated to dealing drugs, which is exactly what I was doing the day she almost lost her life.

It was Senior Skip Day for the graduating class, an informal day for seniors to miss school and blow off a bit of steam before their ultimate release from high school. For our high school, this usually meant a huge party with several kegs out in the woods.

My girlfriend wanted to go and wanted me there as well, but I had arranged a huge drug sale with a guy who was driving over from Denver that day, and I had to wait around for him while she headed to the party alone. We had arranged for her to come and pick me up a few hours later.

So that's what she did. After a few hours of drinking and doing drugs, my girlfriend got in her car and set off to pick me up. I sat on the front porch waiting, and waiting, and waiting. Finally the phone rang and her mother told me that she had run a red light and plowed into a trailer truck. She had driven her car right under it at sixty miles per hour. Had her car been inches taller, it would have taken her head off, but she had managed to escape with only traumatic damage to her face and internal bleeding.

I went to visit her that day in the Intensive Care Unit, and her face was unrecognizable. She told me that they expected that it would take approximately seven surgeries to put her back together. She had tubes and cords coming off her body in all directions—adding fluids here, removing them there, monitoring every single event that was taking place in her poor mangled body. It was truly terrible.

The next day I snuck her some marijuana, just to help bring her spirits up. In fact, I was able to sneak her pot several times before a nurse finally caught us and brought an end to it. We had learned nothing.

A few months later, we finally broke up when she came to a party and made a scene because she was pregnant for the second time. I told her that I didn't believe that the baby was mine, even though I knew it was. That was the end of our high-school romance.

I continued on to become a drug dealer and a bank robber; she ended up shacking up with a drug addict who beat her on a regular basis. Each of us had been stars at one time, athletes, college bound. With drugs running our lives, we were nothing short of pathetic.

•

As an adult today, I can't help but wish I could do more than simply tell this story to the kids that I speak to. I wish that I could make each and every child and teen feel for just one moment what it is like to look back on your life with so much regret.

I said at the beginning of this book that I was supposed to be a ball player. I was supposed to know what it felt like to go to college with other kids and live in a dorm room and take study breaks for pizza. I was supposed to make my mark on the world.

Not for one moment did I think that the first hit that I took off a joint would be the first step to losing it all. In all, I lost twelve and a half years of my life to drugs and seven and a half more to prison. Even today, I can't vote, I can't travel to Australia or New Zealand, I can't own a hunting rifle, and I can't even make a new friend without knowing that at some point I'll have to tell them about my past.

I can't undo the pain that I inflicted on my parents, my friends, my high-school girlfriend, my first wife, or my son. I can't pretend that I wasn't the cause of two abortions or lifetimes of heartache.

All I can do is talk to you now and say *do not* make the same mistakes that I made.

There will always be people who are your so-called "friends" who will encourage you to do things that you know are wrong. Go against the grain and you will risk being called names and treated as an outcast and standing out from the rest of your peers. But then again, why should you care? If they call you names it is only to demonize you, because you have the strength to make a better choice than they did. If they make you feel like an outcast, frankly, you're only an outcast from a group that you probably shouldn't want to belong to anyway. If you stand out from the rest, be proud of it and find a group that shares your values and goals.

High school is tough. Knowing what I know now, I would love to be able to go back and change the decisions that I made, but instead I'm left to live with those choices for the rest of my life. Prison is full of people just like me—the ones who wish that they could change that one key moment in their life when they got off track. Don't let that be you.

Make a choice today to live every day of your life with purpose and the dedication necessary to fulfill your dreams. If you find yourself feeling pressured to do something that you know is self-destructive, listen to that other little voice in the back of your head, the one that tells you to say no. If you need help, ask an adult that you can talk to—a parent, an aunt or uncle, a counselor or teacher—anyone. You may be surprised at how easily they remember facing similar circumstances when they were your age.

Every time you consume any drug—yes, even marijuana or alcohol—you are putting yourself and others at risk. There is no such thing as a safe drug.

Chapter 20

I'm on the Path. Now What Do I Do?

If there be any truer measure of a man than by what he does, it must be by what he gives.

—ROBERT SOUTH

NEVER QUIT GROWING, and use what you've learned to help others.

Once you have found success in one area of your life, you will be amazed at how quickly the rest of your life can fall into place. It is simply a change of attitude. When you take charge of your life and realize that the only thing that can truly hold you back is yourself, you will find that overcoming obstacles is no longer daunting and overwhelming, but simply an everyday exercise that you learn to take in stride. In fact, you might even find that the seemingly unreachable goal you started out with wasn't as much of a reach as you thought, and has merely become a stepping stone on the way to successes you were always too scared to even dream of.

Take my life, for example. I never set out to take on the role or goals that I have today. I wanted to get off drugs, get the education that I had passed by, be the best prison dad that I could be, and try to find honest employment once I was released.

The first item on my list: Get off drugs. That was the easy part. As I had learned in the past, the tough part was staying off them. On the outside, everyday life had proven too stressful for me to quit using drugs, so you can't even imagine how much I craved that release from inside the walls of FCI Englewood. But soon the withdrawals were over and the cravings seemed to ebb. I found that I did, in fact, have the strength to live life without being high, and I was able to gain a momentum through that success that helped to carry me through my darkest hours, when drugs started creeping back into my mind.

Now, I can honestly say that I don't even think of doing drugs anymore. In fact, I've built such a successful lifestyle around being drug-free that it is difficult to imagine that they ever held enough appeal to lure me away from the victories of living a clean life. Better still, I now have the opportunity to be someone who I hadn't dreamed of since junior high—a role model.

Get off drugs and become a role model for those seeking to do the same—check!

List item number two: Get the education that I had passed by. With the system's lack of support for educating convicts beyond obtaining a GED, I was in uncharted territory before I even began my travels. My studies and my education started long before I was awarded my first scholarship. I had to pore over books itemizing scholarship opportunities, hone my writing skills for my applications, and discipline myself to put in the hours I spent writing one application after another, knowing that they would most likely be denied.

Once I received my first scholarship check, however, I was off and running. Not only did I earn the degree that I coveted, but I went on to gain two of them, with straight A's and positions on the Dean's and President's Lists. That was a great success, but the even better one was that I had paved the way for other inmates to do the same. By the time I was transferred out of FCI Englewood, there were several other inmates I had shared my secret with, and as I mentioned earlier, one of them not only obtained his bachelor's degree but also his master's by using the information I had uncovered during my scholarship-funding research.

Obtain degree and help increase future opportunities for my fellow inmates—check!

List item number three: Be the best prison dad I could be. I found out something very important the day that Eric and I had our conversation about my prison sentence. My son loved his dad. It may sound strange to hear that. I think a lot of people take the love of a child that young for granted. I have to say, at that point, I felt like he really just didn't know any better. After all, I was a grown man and much more capable of taking my own tally as a parent than he was. Eric simply had nothing to compare it to at that point. I, on the other hand, lay awake night after night, newly sober, thinking about all of the times I had put that poor kid in harm's way. All the days I hadn't forced myself to put him before my addiction, all the broken promises, all the bad parenting decisions I had ever made came back to me. I had plenty of time to think about them.

While I was on the outside, I knew that I was a terrible father. I had always loved my son, but the drugs and my own insecurities about my parenting abilities always got in the way of making the right decisions. What it all boiled down to was that I was scared of the little guy. He barely came past my waist at that point, but he was terrifying to me. The summers he stayed with me were spent buying him things so he might love me in spite of myself. And every night I fell into bed grateful that I had tricked him for one more day. He hadn't caught on yet.

I suppose that's the amazing thing about a child's love at that age. When I went to prison, I realized for the first time that it never had been about the gifts and the Disneyland Dad act. That little boy loved me just for being his father. I hadn't earned that right yet, but I was going to.

From the moment I was incarcerated, he had my full attention whenever I was with him. I managed to fly him out several times to see me, and I made sure that time was about him—what he wanted to talk about, what he needed—rather than about me. I became invested in his schooling and could actually lead by example for once in my life. As I've said, I wrote him every single day of the seven and a half years that I was inside.

I set out to be the best prison dad that I could be, and in the end, I was a far better father than I ever had been to him when I was on the outside. Now, I look around me at the dads who go through their lives obsessed with "have to" mentalities and I wonder how often they actually pause to think about what a gift it is to have a child. In the end, it's not the money you make, the toys you provide, or the hours you work. None of those things are what earn you points in their eyes. Those are the things that we as adults have assigned importance to. None of that is as valuable to them as ten minutes playing catch with their daddy. Remember to put your role as parent first. There is nothing more special in this world.

Being a father for the first time in my boy's young life and finding out what a gift that truly was—check!

List item number four: Try to find honest employment upon my release. I did it, working at accounting positions found through placement agencies at first, and then as a speaker once I honed my skills in that arena. This is the one item on my list that resulted in returns far beyond anything I had ever dreamed.

I literally wake up every day thankful that I have had the opportunity to become the instrument of change for so many people. I had hoped for a job, but this is so much more. It is a calling.

Gain honest employment in an occupation that lets me make a difference in the world every day of my life—check!

Each of my four goals seemed daunting to me when I first started out. I didn't know how I was going to achieve them, and in the end, the "how" wasn't as important as the fact that I made it to what I had perceived to be the finish line for each and then kept right on going.

This book will be my greatest achievement so far, because it is giving me the opportunity to reach even more people than I could by speaking. This book has helped me to change my perception once again, and I want to share my new goal with you.

My goal is to touch as many lives as I can with my message of encouragement. I am hoping that by this point you are all well on your way to taking your first steps down your own individual path to becoming the person you want to be. As you do that and find you can be successful, and that you are only limited by your own dreams, I want to ask you to join me in bringing this hope to others along the way.

Imagine for just one second if everyone who read this book used it to make a difference in their own lives. And then, if they in turn used their own momentum to share encouragement and the possibility of success with their friends, coworkers, and loved ones.

I originally set out to help change lives, to help others in whatever way that I could. I thought that if I could help just a small fraction of the people who read my book to make positive changes in their lives that I would have done my job. Now, like all of my other goals that I laid out before myself when I went to prison, my original intention has merely become a stepping-stone along the way. To change the lives of a few is an admirable goal, but if I keep spreading my message, and you in turn use it to help others, we could truly touch every soul on the planet.

Imagine what it would be like if there weren't a single person in the

United States, or on Earth, for that matter, who was serving dead time. What could we accomplish then?

I may not be the man I want to be;
I may not be the man I ought to be;
I may not be the man I could be;
I may not be the man I can be;
but praise God, I'm not the man I once was.

—MARTIN LUTHER KING, JR.

About the Author

TROY D. EVANS is a professional speaker and author who resides in Phoenix, Arizona, with his wife Pam and his dog Archibald. Troy travels the country delivering keynote presentations, and since his release from prison has taken the corporate and association platforms by storm with his message about overcoming adversity, adapting to change, and pushing yourself to realize your full potential.

Do you know a group that would benefit from hearing Troy's message? For information on booking Troy, or other available products, please contact:

The Evans Group
3104 E. Camelback Road, #436
Phoenix, AZ 85016
PHONE: 602-265-6855
FAX: 602-285-1474
troy@troyevans.com
www.troyevans.com